Android Programming:
Starting With An App

Mike James

I/O Press
I Programmer Library

ISBN Paperback: 978-1871962475

First Edition
First Printing, 2016
Revision 0

Published by IO Press   www.iopress.info
In association with I Programmer   www.i-programmer.info

Preface

Android™ programming is an attractive proposition. There are more Android users than any other smartphone or tablet and this makes it a potentially huge market. Android devices are relatively cheap and this makes it suitable for implementing smaller scale projects. Finally the tools that you need are free to download and use and you don't need anyone's permission to get started.

The only difficulty is that the Android is a tough system to master. It is easy enough to get started as Android Studio will build you a Hello World app in a few minutes, but what you do next is more difficult. You can get a surprisingly long way in Android programming by simply copying and pasting code from other programs that roughly do what you want, but the results are usually unreliable and disappointing. To create a good app there is no substitute for understanding how the system works and appreciating its strong points and its limitations.

This book aims not only to show you how common tasks are done in Android, but to make sure that you understand why they are done in a particular way. This means covering not just the what but also the why. The good news is that this isn't as difficult as you might expect because Android does have repeating patterns and ways of doing things and once you have seen something in action you find it generalizes to components you haven't encountered.

This isn't a book full of complete examples and case studies. In fact the examples are stripped down to their bare minimum to avoid having to present lines of irrelevant and repetitious code and to let you see what is essential. It also isn't a complete treatment of everything Android. A single book that covered every aspect of the Android system would be too large to pick up and carry. Instead if focuses on the things you need to know to write a simple app. It focuses on creating the user interface (UI) because this is what you spend most of your time working on even if the app in question is sophisticated. At least 90% of the effort in creating any app goes into building and perfecting the UI and this makes it the key place to start. In this book you will find out how to build an app with a single Activity and a UI. If you master this level of the art then you will find it much easier to push on into unknown territory.

It is assumed that you can program, but not necessarily in Java, the language of Android. Java is a very standard object-oriented language and with the help of comments that point out where it is significantly different you should find it easy to pick up as you go along. Finally the development tool used is the latest version of Android Studio because it doesn't make sense not to use it or to use anything else.

This is the place to start.

This book is a revised and updated version of the series of *Android Adventures With Android Studio* on the I Programmer website:

www.i-programmer.info.

There are additional articles on I Programmer that form the basis of the more advanced books that are still in preparation. After updating and revision, *Android Adventures – Mastering Fragments* will be published in print as **Android Programming: Mastering Fragments & Dialogs**. The first draft of **Android Programming: Structuring a Complex App**, which goes further into threading, concurrency, life cycle and other topics crucial to a real world app, is currently work in progress on the website.

To keep informed about forthcoming titles in the **Android Programming** series visit the publisher's website:

www.iopress.info

This is also where you will also find errata, update information to keep up with changes in Android Studio and Android itself and, most importantly, the code from the books. You can also provide feedback to help improve future editions of **Android Programming**.

Table of Contents

Chapter 1

Getting Started With Android Studio

Android represents a big potential market. It is also the most open of the "big" phone and tablet platforms. You can write a program for an Android and let your friends have a copy, keep it to yourself or put it on sale in an app store.

Android phones and tablets are comparatively cheap and this makes it easier to get started. What is even better, all the tools you need to create an Android app are free. You don't need to pay anything to create, or distribute, your Android apps. If you want to sell them using a well known marketplace there may something to pay - there is a one-time fee of $25 to register for Google Play, but you don't have to use any particular distribution method.

All that stands between you and your Android app is your imagination and programming ability. I can't do much to improve your imagination, but I can help with the programming side of things. If you are new to Android programming this is the place to start.

In this book I will show you the fundamentals of Android programming. Not the tips and tricks, but how to think about what is going on. You'll be introduced to the general principles that will make it possible for you to master anything that you encounter that is new in the future. It isn't possible to cover all of Android in one book as the subject is very large. Instead we focus on the basics of creating a User Interface (UI) as all apps have to have some way of interacting with a user.

There are many ways to create an Android app but Google's Android Studio is an easy to use Android IDE - Integrated Development Environment - and it is now the recommended way of doing the job.

Before Android Studio you had to use the Eclipse IDE and setup the SDK and other pieces of software needed. This wasn't difficult, but Android Studio eliminates extra steps and it makes programming Android easy. Put simply, it is the way of the future and so worth your investment in learning it.

With the release of Android Studio Google stopped work on the Eclipse addin and this means that Android Studio really is the only way to develop apps from now on.

You can get started in a few minutes and by the end of this chapter, have your first working Android application.

What You Need to Know

You need to be able to program in a modern object-oriented language. Java would be best as it is the language used to create Android apps, but C++, C#, Visual Basic or anything similar are close enough in spirit to Java for you to be able to cope. You might well need to look things up about the specifics of particular features of Java, but most of the time it should be obvious, or obvious with the help of a few comments.

It isn't necessary to be an expert programmer because for a lot of Android programming you are simply using the features and facilities provided. That is, a lot of Android programming is just a matter of following the rules.

However, if you hope to produce something unique and useful you will at some point have to add something of your own - and here creativity and skill are required. So you might not need to be an expert programmer to get started, but you need to become one by the time you create your amazing app.

Fortunately practice is a good teacher and so learning to make the most of Android Studio will actually help you learn to code.

Making a Start

I'm not going to spend a lot of time explaining how to install Android Studio in a step-by-step way as the Android website does a good job and it is more likely to be up-to-date. It is worth, however, going over the basic principles.

First make sure you have the latest Java JDK installed, at least JDK 6.

If you don't have Java installed visit: https://www.java.com/en/download/ or search for "Java download".

Once you have Java, setting up Android Studio is easy:

Download the Android Studio package from Android Studio Home page:

https://developer.android.com/studio/

Install Android Studio which also installs all of the Android SDK and tools you will need.

Windows:

1. Launch the downloaded EXE file,
    `android-studio-bundle-<version>.exe.`

2. Follow the setup wizard to install Android Studio.

Mac OS X:

1. Open the downloaded DMG file,
   `android-studio-bundle-<version>.dmg`

2. Drag and drop Android Studio into the Applications folder.

Linux:

1. Unpack the downloaded ZIP file,
   `android-studio-bundle-<version>.tgz`,

   into an appropriate location for your applications.

2. To launch Android Studio, navigate to the
   `android-studio/bin/`

   directory in a terminal and execute studio.sh. You may want to add
   `android-studio/bin/`

   to your PATH environmental variable so that you can start Android
   Studio from any directory.

3. Accept any defaults that the setup program offers you - unless you
   have a good reason not to. It installs not only Android Studio, but the
   SDK and the virtual device system that lets you test your application.

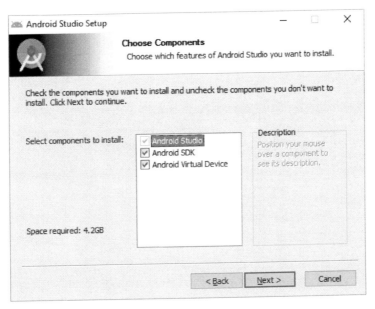

In most cases Android Studio just installs with no problem.

Now you should be able to run Android Studio. If not the most likely cause of
the problem is the JDK and so re-installation is a best first option.

Your First Program

You can opt to start Android Studio after the installation. You will probably not get straight to Android Studio the first time it starts as it downloads updates to itself and to the Android SDK. You just have to be patient.

When it finally gets going you will see the Android Studio welcome screen:

If you have already created some programs you might well see them listed in Recent projects.

Assuming this is your first project select the option:

> Start a new Android Studio project

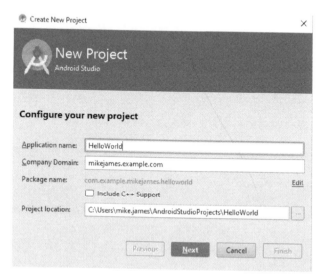

You can ignore the details of the new project for the moment. All you have to do is supply a name for your application - HelloWorld in this case. Accept the other defaults that Android Studio has filled in for you.

When you click Next you are given the chance to pick what devices you are targeting. Again simply accept the defaults:

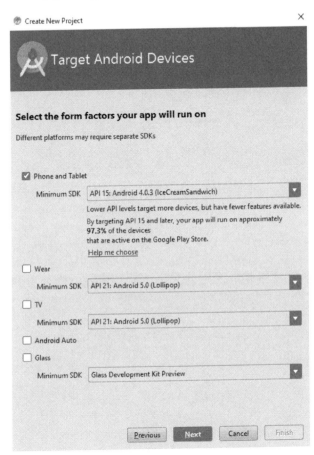

Most of the time you will want to create apps that run on a version of Android that captures the biggest market but if this isn't a concern then it can be better to select a more recent Android version.

The next page lets you select a template for your project. In this case the default Basic Activity is what you need. Every Android application consists of at least one Activity and this template generates a project with a single Activity ready for you to customize.

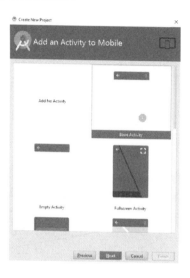

On the next page you can assign custom names for the various components of your project that the template generates. For a real project you would assign names that were meaningful but in this case you can accept the defaults:

Finally you can click the Finish button and wait as Android Studio creates all the files you need. Even a simple Android project has lots of files so again it all takes time.

First Look

When everything is ready you will see Android Studio for the first time. As long as everything has worked you should be presented with a view of your new project starting off in the Designer. Click the Design tab to see the initial user interface:

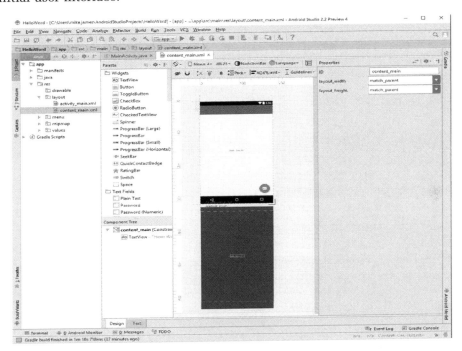

Problems?

If you get any error messages then the chances are that your project hasn't finished being processed. Wait a little while longer for the activity to stop. If you look at the status line at the bottom of the window you will see a message saying "Gradle Build Finished" when Android Studio has finished with your new project.

If you still have problems it is worth trying the **File,Invalidate Caches/Restart** command. This usually works for "Missing styles" and similar errors.

There is a known error that might have been fixed by the time you read this that requires the project to be rebuilt. If you see a rendering error select the menu command **Build, Rebuild Project** You might have to clear the cache again to make it work.

Although there looks like a lot to master in Android Studio's user interface, most of it you will only visit occasionally. The key things to notice are that moving from left to right you have:

- The Project window
- The tool Palette and the Component Tree window
- The Designer
- The Properties window

Most of the time you will be using the Project window and the Properties window. Between the two you will see different editors depending on what sort of file you have selected. In this case you have by default a layout file, **content_main.xml**, selected and hence you have a layout editor in the middle of the screen.

Before we go into layout, which is one of the main topics of this book, it is important that you know a little about the file structure of a project so that you can navigate to its different parts.

Basic Project Structure

When the project has finished building all of the files created can be viewed by opening the Projects tab. The main thing to notice is that there are a great many folders and files.

It seems almost unbelievable that the simplest Android app you can create involves so many files.

Don't panic. Most of the files that have been created are auto-generated and most of the time you don't need to know anything about them, let alone open or edit them. In fact opening and editing auto-generated files really isn't a good idea.

So let's focus on the files that matter to us.

For our simple program there are only two important files. One of them determines the behavior of the Activity:

`MainActivity.java`

The other determines the visual appearance, or View, of the app:

`content_main.xml`

You can set which Activity is the one that the system starts, but by default it is the single activity that you created and named when you set up the project. You can change the default names but for the moment leave them as they are.

The java directory is, from your point of view, where most of the construction of your app occurs so make sure you know where it is. The res directory is where you store all of the resources, layouts, bitmaps, etc, that your app needs.

So while things look complicated at the moment the only two project files that matter to you, and your project, are MainActivity.java in the java folder and content_main.xml in the res folder.

The two other folders in the java folder are concerned with creating tests for your program. This is not something that we need to worry about when first starting to write Android apps.

Anatomy of an Activity

An Android app is made up of one or more Activity classes.

You can think of an Activity as being something like a web page complete with HTML to determine what displays and JavaScript to determine what it does.

In the case of an Activity the layout is determined by the XML file in resource (res) folder, this is often called the View, and the behavior is determined by the Java code in the java folder.

The XML can be thought of as a markup language much like HTML or XAML. It defines an initial layout for the screen when the app first runs. It is possible to generate new layout components at runtime from the Java file. In fact, if you really want to, you can dispense with the XML file and generate everything from Java, but as you will discover the XML markup approach is much the best way to do the job because of the availability of the Designer. So to be 100% clear:

- The java file contains the code that makes your app behave in particular ways,
- The .xml layout file contains a definition of the initial UI, the View, of your app.

Hello Layout Designer

Let's take a look at the two files that have been generated for our initial Hello World application beginning with the XML layout. Double click on content_main.xml file in the Project tab and the file will open (if it isn't already open). If it is already open you can also select its tab displayed just above the editor area. You can select any file that is open for editing by selecting its tab.

You can work with the XML directly to define where all the buttons and text go and later you will learn how to edit it when things go wrong or to fine tune it. However, Android Studio provides you with a very nice interactive editor – the Layout Designer or just "the Designer" and this is worth using.

As you become more experienced the idea of switching between a design view and an XML view will become second nature. Think of the interactive editor as a very easy way of generating the XML that otherwise would take you ages to get right. If you look at the bottom left you will see two tabs - Design and Text:

You can switch between editing the XML as text and editing it in the drag-and-drop designer simply by clicking on the tab. If you now click on the tab the window will display the Designer but be patient the first time you do this it might take a few moments.

The Designer looks a little too much to take in when you first see it but you will quickly get used to it. On the left is a Palette of all of the components or controls - buttons, text, checkboxes and so on - that you can place on the design surface:

In the middle is the design surface and this defaults to the screen size and appearance of the Nexus 5. You can select other devices to work with. The two displays of the layout, which are either one above the other or side by side, show you an actual layout view and a design overview, referred to as the blueprint.

For a simple application the blueprint view isn't necessary and in most cases it is better to recover the space it occupies for the actual layout. To remove the blueprint view all you have to do is click on the icon at the top left of the design area:

On the left, below the Palette, you have the Component Tree which shows you the structure of your layout, that is how different UI components are contained inside others. It shows you the structure of the XML file in an easier to use form. You can use the Component Tree as an easy way of to select individual UI components by clicking on their names.

On the right you have the Properties window that can be used to set the properties, such as width, height, color and so on of any component in the layout. If you have used any drag-and-drop designer then this will seem familiar and if you have struggled with detailed layout using a markup language. be it HTML, XAML or XML, you will appreciate how easy the designer makes building and testing a UI.

In the case of our sample program the only component is a single TextView already containing the text "Hello World". A TextView is the standard component to use when all we want to do is to display some static text.

You can modify the greeting text if you want to. Select the TextView component either on the Nexus 5 image or in the Component Tree and use the Properties window to find its Text property. Change this to read "Hello Android World".

You can use the designer to create any UI you care to and you really don't have to get involved in the XML that corresponds to the layout - unless things go wrong or you need to do something so sophisticated that the designer doesn't support it.

Inspecting the XML

The designer will automatically generate the XML needed to create the layout for you and modify it as you change the layout. If you really want to see the XML then all you have to do is select the Text tab at the bottom of the designer window.

```xml
<?xml version="1.0" encoding="utf-8"?>
<RelativeLayout xmlns:android=
      "http://schemas.android.com/apk/res/android"
xmlns:app="http://schemas.android.com/apk/res-auto"
xmlns:tools="http://schemas.android.com/tools"
android:id="@+id/content_main"
android:layout_width="match_parent"
android:layout_height="match_parent"
android:paddingBottom="@dimen/activity_vertical_margin"
android:paddingLeft="@dimen/activity_horizontal_margin"
android:paddingRight="@dimen/activity_horizontal_margin"
android:paddingTop="@dimen/activity_vertical_margin"
app:layout_behavior="@string/appbar_scrolling_view_behavior"
tools:context="com.example.mikejames.helloworld.MainActivity"
tools:showIn="@layout/activity_main">
<TextView
  android:layout_width="wrap_content"
  android:layout_height="wrap_content"
  android:text="Hello Android World!" />
</RelativeLayout>
```

You should find it fairly easy to understand - read the <TextView> tag for example - but leave it to the designer to create and modify it. The quantities starting with @ are all references to things defined elsewhere in resource files, more of this in a later chapter.

We will return to the designer and the XML it generates later.

The Java

If you double click on the MainActivity.java file, or just select the MainActivity.java tab, you will see the code it contains. Some of the code might hidden but you can inspect it if you want to by clicking the + buttons to expand it.

The important part of the code is:

```
public class MainActivity extends AppCompatActivity
@Override
protected void onCreate(Bundle savedInstanceState) {
 super.onCreate(savedInstanceState);
 setContentView(R.layout.activity_main);
```

You can ignore the instructions that follow the setContentView function because these set up the standard "extras" that every Android application now supports - a floating ActionBar.

There are two other functions below the onCreate function but ignore these for the moment. They implement features you didn't really ask for which can be useful, but not when you are just getting started.

The **onCreate** function is the only thing that matters at the moment. This function is called when your app is run and it is expected to create the view and do the actions the Activity is concerned with.

As our Activity doesn't really do anything much the only thing onCreate has to do is first call the inherited OnCreate method, **super.onCreate**, to do all the standard things and then use the **setContentView** function to select the XML file that determines the layout of the Activities screen.

The line:

```
 setContentView(R.layout.activity_main);
```

is the most important of all and really the only one that actually does anything. It gets the resource object that represents the layout as defined by the XML file created by the designer and makes it the current ContentView, i.e. it is what is displayed on the screen. In other words, it makes the connection between the layout you have defined using the designer and stored in the XML file and the user interface that appears on the device's screen.

You may be puzzled as to why you edited a resource file called **content_main.xml** and yet the Java is loading a resource file called **activity_main.xml**

The answer is that to make extending your app easier Android Studio creates two layout files, activity_main.xml that creates the "standard" controls that are displayed and content_main.xml that you use to design your custom UI. Of course, activity_main.xml contains a reference to content_main.xml. This makes things more complicated for the beginner but it is a simplification later.

We have more to learn about the resource object R but you can see that its main role is to form a link between your Java code and the resources that have been created as XML files by the designer.

As this is all our Activity does this is all the code we need. While I agree it is hardly an "activity" it is enough to see the basic outline of an Android app and to see how to get it running - which is our next job.

Getting Started with the Emulator

There are two distinct ways of running an Android app using Android Studio. You can use the emulator or a real Android device. Eventually you will have to discover how to run an app on a real connected Android device because the emulator only allows you to test a subset of things and it is slow. However, for the moment running your first app on an emulator is quite enough to get started.

All you have to do is click the green run icon in the top toolbar - or use the Run,Run "app" menu item. When you do this for the first time it will take a while for the app to be compiled. Subsequent runs are much faster due to optimizations introduced in Android Studio 2.

When your app is ready to be compiled you will see a dialog box appear which allows you to either select a running emulator or start one going.

If no emulators are listed then you will have to create one. Select the Create New Emulator button. This will present a dialog box where you can select the device you want to test on. The default is the Nexus 5 and for a first test you might as well use this. If you need other devices you can use the AVD (Android Virtual Device) Manager to define them.

You can accept all of the defaults in this first run. You can monitor the loading of the emulation in the Run window which appears automatically at the bottom of Android Studio. You may see some warnings appear - these can mostly be ignored.

The whole process takes some time the first time you do it. After the first time the emulator is already running and the instant run feature tries to re-run your app with the minimum changes.

Finally, remember to wait until the Android operating system is loaded and you see the familiar home screen before you start to wonder where your app is. Even when it is loaded it is a good idea to give it a few seconds for Android Studio to notice it and to upload your app.

In our case this isn't particularly impressive - just the words "Hello Android World!", but when you think of the journey traveled it really should impress.

From this point you can now modify the code or the layout and run the app again to see the effects of the changes. If anything goes wrong and you get in a mess then simply delete the project and create it again from scratch.

You still have a lot to discover about how to extend the app and make it useful, but the adventure has begun.

Summary

- Android Studio makes creating Android apps a lot easier than other approaches and it is currently the only official way to do the job.

- An app has at least one Activity and this defines a screen layout, the View, and a behavior. An Activity doesn't have to have a UI, but in most cases it does have one.

- To create a simple application use the Basic Activity template with no extras selected.

- The screen layout is controlled by an XML markup file, Main_Activity.xml, stored in the res directory. There is also content_main.xml, which is where we place our custom UI controls.

- Android Studio provides a drag-and-drop designer that allows you to create a UI without having to work directly with the XML.

- The behavior of the app is controlled by a Java file, MainActivity.java in our case stored, in the java folder. You can edit the code in the Java file directly in Android Studio. The Java code has to load and display the layout defined in the XML file.

- To run an app you need either an emulator based AVD or a real Android device connected to the machine.

- When you run the app you can select which AVD or which hardware device is used to test it. When you first start simply use the default AVD, a Nexus 5.

- You can modify and re-run your app without having to restart the AVD or any real hardware connected to the machine.

Chapter 2

Activity and User Interface

So you know how to create an Android app, but do you really know how it works? In this chapter we look at how to create a user interface (UI) and how to hook it up to the code in the Activity.

We discovered in Chapter 1 how to use Android Studio to build the simplest possible app. On the way we discovered that an Android app consists of two parts - an Activity and a View. The Activity is the Java code that does something and the View provides the user interface (UI). You can think of this duality as being similar to the HTML page and the JavaScript that runs to make it do something, or as a XAML form and the code behind.

The key idea is that an Activity is the code that works with a UI screen defined by the View. This isn't quite accurate in that an Activity can change its view so that one chunk of Java code can support a number of different views. However, there are advantages to using one Activity per view because, for example, this how the Android back button navigates your app - from Activity to Activity.

A complex app nearly always consists of multiple Activities that the user can move between like web pages but a simple app can manage quite well with just one Activity. There is no hard and fast rule as to how many Activities your app has to have, but it has to have least one.

If you are wondering if an Activity can exist without a View the answer is that it can, but it doesn't make much sense as this would leave the user with no way to interact with your app. Activities are active when their View is presented to the user.

It really is a great simplification to think in terms of an Activity as a single screen with a user interface.

If you want something to run without a UI then what you want is a service or a content provider which is beyond the scope of this book.

It is also worth making clear at this early stage that an Activity has only one thread of execution - the UI thread - and you need to be careful not to perform any long running task because this would block the UI and make your app seem to freeze. That is, an Activity can only do one thing at a time and this includes interacting with the user. If you write a program using a single activity and it does a complicated calculation when the user clicks a button then the activity will not be able to respond to any additional clicks or anything that happens in the UI until it finishes the calculation.

In most cases the whole purpose of the Activity that it associated with the UI is to look after the UI and this is what this book is mostly about.

Also notice that creating additional Activities doesn't create new threads. Only one Activity is active at any given time, more of this later when we consider the Activity lifecycle in detail.

In this book we are going to concentrate on the single screen UI Activity because it is the most common app building block you will encounter and it is even where most complex apps start from.

The MainActivity

There is one activity in every project that is nominated as the one to be launched when your app starts. If you use Android Studio to create a new Basic Activity app called **SimpleButton** and accept all the defaults, the startup Activity is called MainActivity by default. You can change which Activity starts the app by changing a line in the app's manifest.

The Manifest is a project file we haven't discussed before because if you are using Android Studio you can mostly ignore it and allow Android Studio to construct and maintain it for you, but it is better if you know it exists and what it does.

The Manifest is stored in the app/manifests directory and is called AndroidManifest.xml.

It is an XML file that tells the Android system everything it needs to know about your app, including what permission it requires to run on a device.

In particular it lists all of the activities and which one is the one to use to start the app.

If you open the generated Manifest, by double-clicking on it, you will see a little way down the file:

```
<activity
 android:name=".MainActivity"
 android:label="SimpleButton" >
```

This defines the Activity the system has created for you and the lines just below this define it as the startup Activity:

```
<intent-filter>
  <action android:name="android.intent.action.MAIN" />
  <category android:name="android.intent.category.LAUNCHER" />
  </intent-filter>
</activity>
```

Notice that the choice of which Activity starts the app has nothing to do with what you call it, i.e. calling it MainActivity isn't enough.

For the moment you can rely on Android Studio to look after the Manifest for you. In most cases you will only need to edit it directly when you need to correct an error or add something advanced.

Inside the Activity

The generated Activity has one class, **MainActivity**, which holds all of the methods and properties of your activity.

It also have three generated methods -

- onCreate
- onCreateOptionsMenu
- onOptionsItemSelected

The last two are obviously connected to the working of the **OptionsMenu**, which is an important topic but one that can be ignored for the moment. Not all Activities need to have an OptionsMenu and you could even delete these methods if you don't want to support an options menu.

All three of these methods are event handlers. That is they are called when the event that they are named after occurs. The whole of an Android app is a collection of nothing but event handlers and their helper functions.

The most important method generated by Android Studio is onCreate. This is an event handler and it is called when your app is created and is where we do all the initialization and setting up for the entire app. It is also generally the place we show the app's main UI screen.

Let's take another look at the first two lines of generated code for onCreate, which are the most important:

```
protected void onCreate(Bundle savedInstanceState) {
  super.onCreate(savedInstanceState);
  setContentView(R.layout.activity_main);
```

The onCreate event handler is passed a Bundle object called savedInstanceState. This is intended to preserve state information between invocations of your app and we will see how this is used later. In this case no data has been saved and so savedInstanceState is null - but you still have to pass it on to the inherited onCreate method. You will learn a lot more about Bundle in Chapter 12.

The final instruction calls setContentView, which is a method that has a number of different overloaded forms. In this case we pass an integer that indicates which XML file describes the layout to be used for the view. The setContentView method uses this to create all of the components of your UI as defined in the XML file. That is, this is the connection between the layout you created using the designer and the layout that appears on the device's screen.

It is worth looking a little closer at the way that the layout file is specified because this is a general way that Android lets you access resources. There is a whole chapter about resources later but it is still worth an introduction now.

The R object is constructed by the system to allow you to access the resources you have placed in the resource directories. For example, in onCreate the use of R.layout.activity_main returns an integer value, its id, that allows the setContentView method to find the activity_main XML layout file. In general all resources are found via the R object, think of it as an index of resources.

View and ViewGroup

So far so good, but it is important to realize that what happens next it that the XML file is rendered as a set of View objects. That is, Java objects that are all sub-classes of the View object. The entire UI and graphics system is implemented as a hierarchy of components derived from the View class. If you have used almost any GUI framework, AWT, Swing, XAML, etc, this idea will not be new to you. For example, a button is a class derived from View and to create a button all you have to do is create an instance of the Button class. You can, of course create as many buttons as you like simply by creating more instances.

This leaves open the question of where the button appears in the layout?

The answer to this is that there are ViewGroup objects which act as containers for other View objects. You can set the position of the child View objects or just allow them to be controlled by various layout rules, more of which later. You can opt to create the entire UI in code by creating and working with instances of View objects and this is something demonstrated in Chapter 7.

So to be 100% clear all of the UI objects are defined in code and every UI object, such as a button, has a Java class with a similar name that lets you create the UI in code. In fact this is the only way to create the UI, but there are other ways of specifying it. Instead of writing code to create the UI you can specify what you want in an XML file and then use supplied code to display it. This is what setContentView does - it reads the XML file you specify and creates Java objects that implement the UI.

This means you could create the UI by manually writing an XML file that defines view objects and how they nest one within another and rely on the system to create the view object hierarchy for you. Although this is possible, it is much easier to use the designer to create the XML file and then allow the system to create the objects for you from the generated XML file. That is, you can drag-and-drop a button onto the designer and it will automatically generate the XML needed to create it and specify where it is and all of the other details you set.

That is, at the surface level there are three ways to create the UI.

1. You can write Java code to generate the necessary Java objects.

2. You can write XML tags and use the system to convert the XML to the same Java objects.

3. You can use the designer to interactively create the UI and generate the XML file which is then converted into the Java objects needed. You can think of this as:

```
drag-and-drop layout -> XML -> Java View objects
```

Being able to work with the UI in an interactive editor is one of the great advantages of using Android Studio and, even if you know how to edit the XML layout file directly, it isn't a feature you should ignore. It is nearly always a good idea to use the layout editor as the first step and apply any tweaks, if necessary, to the XML file later.

Creating Our First UI

To see how all of this fits together let's add a button and a textView object.

You probably already know that a button is for pressing and you can guess that a textView is used to show the user some text.

First remove the Hello World text that is generated automatically when you create a new blank Activity. Load the content_main.xml file by opening it from the project view.

The content_main.xml is where you create all of your UI. There is another layout file, but as explained in Chapter 1 this simply provides the standard elements in a UI like the AppBar. Notice that because of this you can see UI components in the designer that you cannot edit - they belong to the other layout file.

To remove "Hello World" all you have to do is select it and press the delete key:

Notice that there is an undo command, Ctrl-Z, if you delete something by mistake.

Next select the button in the Widgets section of the Palette by clicking on it:

If you now place the cursor over the design area you will discover that as you move it various alignments are indicated by lines:

To position the button simply click and a full button, complete with the default caption Button, will appear.

Now you have a button on the UI, let's add a TextView in exactly the same way. Simply click on it in the Palette, position it in the designer and click it to set its position.

Notice that Android Studio provides positioning information to help you align components of the UI:

That's about it and in fact creating a complete complex UI is just more of the same, just a matter of picking components from the Palette and positioning them on the design surface.

If you now run the program, by clicking the green Run icon (refer back to Chapter 1 if you don't know how to do this) you will see your new UI:

Of course it doesn't do anything, even if you can click the button. The button does click, but there is no code connected to the button click event to say what should happen, something we will deal with very soon.

Properties

Our next task is to change the caption on the button. Recall that objects have properties and methods. Things like caption text, background color and so on for UI widgets are represented as properties. You can change properties in code or at design time you can use the Properties window on the right-hand side of the screen.

If you select the button and examine the Properties window on the right you will find the button's text property. This currently contains the value "Button". If you change this to "Click Me!" and re-run the app you will see that the Button's caption has changed.

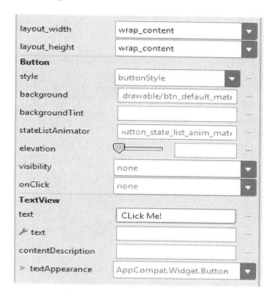

You can set the initial properties of any of the widgets that you have placed in the UI. There are a great many properties and we need to spend some time looking at some of them. However, for the moment the important thing is that you see how easy it is to change a property using the Properties window.

As you might guess, the property that you changed results in a change in the XML file defining the layout. Recall that the general principle is that the Designer creates the XML file that you could have created by hand without any help from the Designer. In this sense, the Designer doesn't add anything to the process, other than being much easier.

Events

Now we want to do something when the button is clicked. Android supports a complete event-driven UI. So what we need to do next is define a method, or function, that is called when the button is clicked.

If you are familiar with other languages you might find the Java way of working with events strange and convoluted. It is and we will have to come back to discover the full story of how events are implemented later.

There are a number of different ways to specify an event handler, but the simplest is to use the designer to generate the XML needed for the system to hookup the event handler to the event. This is not an approach that you can use all of the time. It only works for the click event, but it gets you started.

If you have used something like Visual Studio, it is also worth pointing out that Android Studio doesn't automatically create event handlers for you. In the case of Android Studio you have to create a function and then assign it as the onClick handler. The reason for this apparently unhelpful approach is that Java events are much more involved than .NET or JavaScript events.

Using the designer approach, method click event handlers are simply public methods of the current Activity with the signature:

```
void method( View v)
```

Just in case you have missed or forgotten what a function's signature is:

A functions signature is the number and types of the parameters it accepts. Functions with the same name but different signatures are considered to be different functions. In this case the function takes a single parameter, which is a View, and returns void, i.e. nothing.

You can call the method anything you like, but in most cases it helps to specify exactly what the event it handles is. In this case we want to handle the button's onClick event - which occurs when the user clicks on the button with a mouse or more likely taps on the button using a touch sensitive device.

Load the MainActivity.java file into the code editor and add the following method:

```
public void buttonOnClick(View v) {
  // do something when the button is clicked
}
```

This needs to be added directly following the onCreate method or anywhere that makes it a method of the MainActivity class.

With all this code out of the way, now switch back to the Designer, select the button, find the onClick property in the Properties Window to enter or select buttonOnClick:

Notice that you don't type in parameters, just the name of the method. If you enter the click event handler before you try to set the property then you will find that it is in the drop-down list that appears when you click the down arrow on the right.

There is a bug in Android Studio 2.2.2 that adds the class that the event handler is in to its property value. That is it shows in the onClick property as buttonOnClick(MainActivity). The bug is that this is the string used in the XML

```
android:onClick="onClick (MainActivity)"
```

and this is incorrect as it tries to call onClick with a parameter MainActivity. You have to edit this out so that the XML reads

```
android:onClick="onClick"
```

That's all there is to it. You define your event handler with the correct signature and return type and set the appropriate onClick property in the Properties window.

When it comes to other types of event you have to do the job in code - the XML/Designer method only works for onClick.

Connecting the Activity to the UI

Now we have an event handler hooked up to the button click event we usually want to do something that affects the UI as a result.

Let's suppose that when the button is clicked we want to change the text displayed in the TextView widget to "You Clicked Me!".

We can do this by changing the TextView widget's text property to the new text. The only problem is how do we find the TextView widget in code?

This is a fairly standard problem when you use a markup language to define a UI. The markup language defines widgets, or other UI objects, and the code has to have a way of making the connection to those UI objects. For example, in JavaScript you make use of the getElementById method to retrieve a DOM object corresponding to a particular HTML element.

In Android we do something similar.

First make sure you follow the idea that all of the XML generated by the designer gets converted into a set of Java objects, one for each component or View placed on the design surface. These objects have the same range of properties as you saw in the Properties window and have methods to get other things done. All you need to do if find a way to reference one of them.

In the case of the View object that caused the event this is very easy as it is passed to the event handler as the only argument of the call. So if the event handler is:

```
public void buttonOnClick(View v) {
```

and the event handler is only hooked up to the button, then you can be 100% sure that v is the button object when the event occurs.

If you want to change the button's caption you could just use its setText method to change its value.

Note: if you aren't used to Java then it is worth pointing out that generally all Java frameworks follow the rule that if an object has a property called myProperty, visible as such in the Properties window, then in code you set it using setMyProperty and retrieve it using getMyProperty.

So, in principle, all you have to write is:

```
v.setText("I've Been Clicked!");
```

However, this doesn't work because v is declared to be a general View object which doesn't have a setText method - not all View objects have text to set.

To call the Button's setText method we have to cast v to its correct type, namely a Button.

Note: Casting is where you tell the system the type of the object you are working with. If classB is a subclass of classA then you can treat a classB object as a classA - after all it has all of the methods and properties that classA does by inheritance. However, if you want to make use of a property or method that only classB has then you need to cast the reference to the classB object to make its type clear.

For example, assuming classB inherits from classA:

```
classA myObject = new classB();
```

creates an instance of classB but myObject is declared to be of type classA. This is fine but you can only access the methods and properties of the classA object.

However, if you try:

```
myObject.classBMethod();
```

then it will fail if classBMethod only exists in classB. To use the classB method you have to cast myObject to its real type:

```
(classB) myObject
```

You can store a reference to the cast in a new variable:

classB myClassBObject = (classB) myObject;

and then call the method

myClassBObject.classBMethod();

or you can just do the cast on the fly at the cost of an extra pair of parentheses:

((classB) myObject).classBMethod();

If you simply change the code to cast the v object to a Button object, i.e. (Button)v, you will discover that Android Studio flags an error by showing Button in red. If you hover over the red symbol you will see the exact error message:

```
public void buttonOnClick(View v) {
    Button button=(Button) v;          }
```
Cannot resolve symbol 'Button'

This is because you have used a class without importing it.

In Java any class that you use has to be listed at the top of the program in an import statement. Whenever you see a "Cannot resolve symbol" error message the most likely cause is that you haven't imported the class.

This can be a tedious business but Android Studio has some help for you. If you click on the error symbol you will see a blue hint message:

```
? android.widget.Button? Alt+Enter
        public void buttonOnClick(View v) {
            Button button=(Button) v;
```

If you look at the hint message it suggests pressing Alt+Enter which is always good advice because it produces a list of possible fixes for the problem.

You can implement the fix simply by selecting it from the list.

In this case you have to add the class definition to the start of the program.

```
import android.widget.Button;
```

You can do this manually, i.e. you can type it in, or just select the first option. The import is added and in a moment the red errors disappear.

If you hover over the corrected Button class name you will also see a light bulb.

Android Studio offers you hints on improving your code even when there are no errors - look out for the light bulbs. If you click on this one it will offer to split the declaration and the assignment as being better style. Android Studio is full of hints and offers to make your code better at every turn - you don't have to accept them.

For the moment let's stick with the single line.

```
Button button=(Button) v;
```

Now we have the button object we can call its setText method:

```
button.setText("I've Been Clicked!");
```

The complete event handler is:

```
public void buttonOnClick(View v) {
 Button button=(Button) v;
 button.setText("I've Been Clicked!");
}
```

Now if you run the program you will see the button's caption change when you click the button.

This is a common pattern in making your UI work - event handlers change the properties of View objects to modify the UI. Notice that this approach only works if you know the type of the object that caused the event and called the event handler. If your event handler is only connected to a single component then you do know the type of the object that caused the event. If it isn't, or if you want to modify the properties of a View object that isn't the subject of the event, then you have to find it. This is exactly what we are going to do next.

Finding View Objects

Now suppose we want to do something to one of the other components in the View. In this case we have to find the object that represents the component without the help of the event handler's argument. For example how do we find the TextView that we placed below the button?

In the event handler the Button is the object that caused the event to happen so it is already found, but how do you find another component in the layout?

This is a very standard pattern in working with View objects from the Activity. First you make use of the R object to find the component's id. In this case the TextView has been given the id textView by default so we can use:

```
R.id.textView:
```

and this returns a unique integer that identifies the component.

Next we use the Activity's

```
findViewById(int)
```

method which takes the integer id and returns the Java object corresponding to id.

Of course this is returned as a View object because findViewById doesn't know the type of the object it returns any more accurately. So we have to cast to make use of the TextView object.

Putting all this together gives:

```
TextView myTextView=(TextView) findViewById(R.id.textView);
```

Once again Android Studio will complain about TextView and if you press Alt+Enter it will add the class import to the start of the program for you:

```
import android.widget.TextView;
```

Now that you have the TextView object you can use the setText method to change what it displays:

```
myTextView.setText("You Clicked My Button!");
```

The complete event handler is:

```
public void buttonOnClick(View v) {
  Button button=(Button) v;
  button.setText("I've Been Clicked!");
  TextView myTextView=(TextView)findViewById(R.id.textView);
  myTextView.setText("You Clicked My Button!");
}
```

If you now run the program you will see that you are informed twice of the fact that this very important button has been clicked:

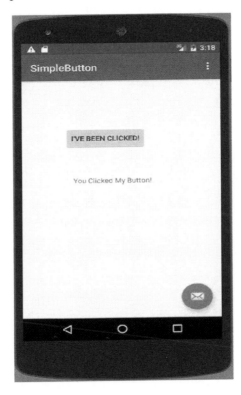

You may think that this is all very small stuff and nothing like a real app, but this is how building a UI works in Android.

You now know how to design a single screen app using the widgets available in the Designer's Toolbox and how to hook them up to handle their click events, find the Java object that represents them and how to call methods that modify them.

Apart from the fine detail of how each of the widgets works - radio buttons, checkboxes and so on - you now have the general outline of how to build a single screen app.

Summary

- An Activity is the unit of the Android app and it roughly corresponds to one screenful of user interface plus the code to make it work.

- In most cases you will create an Activity for each UI screen you want to present to your user.

- Only one Activity from your app is running at any given time.

- An Activity is single-threaded and runs on the UI thread.

- You can set which Activity starts the app in the Manifest. Android Studio sets this to MainActivity by default.

- The Activity has events corresponding to different stages in its lifecycle. The onCreate event is called when the app first starts and this is where you perform all initialization.

- You can also restore the apps state from previous runs at this point.

- The Activity then loads a View or ViewGroup object to create its user interface.

- You can create View/ViewGroup objects in three possible ways: in code, using XML or using the designer to generate the XML.

- The designer is far the easiest way to create a UI.

- By opening the XML file you can use the designer to place widgets corresponding to View objects on the design surface.

- You can use the property window to set the properties of each widget.

- The XML file that the designer creates is used by the Activity to set its UI by creating Java objects that correspond to each of the View objects placed using the designer.

- When you reference a class that isn't defined in the file, i.e. most of them, then you need to add an import statement to the start of the code.

- If you use Alt+Enter when the cursor is positioned within any word that is displayed in red then Android Studio will help you fix the problem.

- You can hook up onClick event handlers defined within the current Activity to the widgets using the Properties window.
- An onClick event handler is just a public function with the signature void myEventHandler(View v)
- The View object parameter is sent to the View object that raised the event. This can be used to access the properties/methods of the View object that the user interacted with.
- To access other View objects you follow the standard pattern of:
  1. Find the integer id via the string id, set in the designer, of the widget using resource object R.id.stringId.
  2. Use the integer id to retrieve the Java object corresponding to the widget using findViewById(int Id)
  3. Work with the object's methods/properties to modify it.

Chapter 3

Building a Simple UI

By this point in you understand how the Activity and the View fit together to create a simple application, but the Android UI is more complicated than most because of its need to cope with a range of very different screen sizes and orientations. In this chapter we look at the problem of layout and working with the UI framework and on the way we'll build a calculator app.

When building an Android app you will spend far more time than you could possibly imagine on perfecting the UI. So it is important that you master the basics so that you can move on to code that does more interesting things.

The learning curve with any UI framework is more or less the same. First you have to find out what constitutes an application that you can run i.e. where is the code? In Android's case this is an Activity.

Next you have to work out how UI components are represented, how you can create them and how to hook up the UI with the code. In Android's case this is a matter of a hierarchy of View objects and hooking up with the code is a matter of finding the objects representing each UI component and adding event handlers.

Once you have the basics you have to start exploring what components you have been provided with to build a UI. In general this vary from the extremely simple - the Button, for example - to almost complete applications in themselves - the Listview, for example. It would take a long time to master all of them, but what most programmers do is make sure that they can use the basic components and then find out about the bigger more sophisticated components when needed. The good news is that once you know how one component, even the simplest, works then most of it generalizes to bigger more complicated things.

We also have to worry about how to lay out the UI - how to size and position and sets of components. Android is particularly sophisticated in this respect because being a mobile operating system it has to contend with a wide range of screen sizes and even orientation changes while an app is running. This is not a simple topic and we will have to consider it in more detail later, but for the moment let's just take a look at the easier aspects of screen layout.

Using the Designer is the simplest and most productive way to work so let's continue to concentrate on this method of creating a UI. This chapter is mostly about how to use the Designer with the default layout and the challenges of creating a UI.

What's In The Palette

Start Android Studio and create a new simple basic activity project called **Uitest**. This is going to be our UI playground for the rest of this chapter. Accept all the defaults, apart from selecting a Basic Activity, and wait while the project is created.

If you now open the file content_main.xml in the app/res/layout folder then the Designer will open and you will see the familiar rendering of the default layout. Now it is time to look at the Palette in more detail:

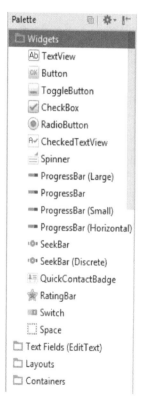

The top four sections of the Palette hold the most important UI components with a further five sections with more specialized ones.

1. The Widgets section contains the most frequently used components - Buttons, TextViews, Checkboxes and so on. This is the set of components you need to learn to use first.

2. Text Fields are a set of text input components which all work in more or less the same way.

3. Layouts are containers for other components that provide different layout rules.

4. Containers which are like mini-layouts in that you generally put other components inside them and the container "looks after" them.

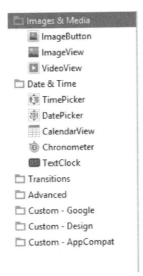

5. Images and media are containers for specific types of resources such as images and videos.

6. Date and time are widgets concerned with data and time entry and display

7. Transitions perform limited animation between different components

8. Advanced doesn't really mean advanced - more bigger and complex components such as the number picker

9. Custom consists of three division Google, Design and App Compat. It is mostly a collection of widgets that don't belong elsewhere.

The Button An Example

Where else should we start - the Button is almost the "Hello World" of UI construction. If you know how to work with a Button you are well on your way to understanding all of the possible components. The good news is that we have already met and used the Button in Chapter 2 and discovered how to work with it in code. However, there is still a lot to find out.

Generally there are three things you need to discover about using any component.

1. How to make it initially look like you want it to. This is a matter of discovering and setting properties using the Designer.
1. How to modify the way a component looks at runtime. This is a matter of finding out how to work with properties in code.
2. How to hook up the events generated by the component to the code.

Setting properties sounds easy, but there are different types of properties and these have different appropriate ways of allowing you to interact with them.

The first thing we have to find out about is how to position a component.

Positioning Relative To The Parent

Before you continue with the project, select and delete the default "hello world" text as it makes trying things out easier to have a clean design surface. Next click on the Button in the palette and drag it to the design surface, noticing the way the layout information changes as you move the button around the design surface. You can see arrows provided to show you what the button is positioned relative to. As you move the button the arrows are drawn to the closest other UI component, in this case the edge of the screen:

It is worth saying that the RelativeLayout is the most sophisticated of the "classic" Layouts. In Android Studio 2.2 the Constraint Layout was introduced with the idea of replacing the RelativeLayout. More about this in a later chapter but for now we will stay with the RelativeLayout because it is still useful. There are other simpler Layouts and we will return to this wider topic in Chapter 6.

In RelativeLayout components are positioned relative to other components. When you start the only other component is the layout itself and so you are essentially positioning relative to the layout container, i.e. the whole screen.

The RelativeLayout only supports nine different positions for a component:

- Top — left, center and right
- Center — left, center and right
- Bottom — left ,center and right

All components are positioned at one of these nine locations and you can see the arrows drawn to the left, right, top or bottom as you move the component about. To provide a finer positioning you can specify an offset in terms of a margin which you can see as the size of the arrows. In other words, you are positioning components at say the top left of the screen but then by setting a left margin of 20 and a top margin of 30 you can move the component to the exact position you want, i.e. 20,30. This combination of one of the nine fixed positions in the layout plus continuously variable margins work together to allow you to place a component anywhere on the design surface. If you play with the positioning in the Designer you will quickly get the idea.

As you might guess, there are properties which let you set the location and margins for each position manually. All layout properties start with layout_name where the name gives the positioning performed. For example, if you click View all properties in the Properties window you will see:

```
layout_alignParentTop
layout_alignParentLeft
layout_alignParentRight
layout_alignParentBottom
```

and

```
layout_centerInParent
layout_centerVertical
layout_centerHorizontal
```

You can see that a combination of these plus:

```
layout_margin
```

gives you all of the positioning possibilities we have seen in the Designer.

Each property can be set to true or false. If you don't include the property in the XML file then it is assumed to be false. You can can set the properties using the Properties window. A tick sets the property to true, a blank is false and a minus removes the property from the XML file.

Notice that not all settings of these properties make sense - e.g. saying you want the component at the top and centered vertically doesn't make sense. Some do make sense if you interpret them correctly. For example, setting alignParentLeft and alignParentRight aligns the left side of the control with the left side of the container and the right side of the control with the right side of the container, i.e. it changes the control's width.

It is also worth understanding that, in allowing you to set the position of a component by simply dragging it to the location you want, the Designer is working out how to set multiple properties correctly. You could do this manually to get the same effect, but the Designer takes where you have positioned a component relative to other controls and the container and works out how to set the properties. This is why it is easier to let the Designer set the properties for you.

Relative To Another Control

Positioning in a relative layout with respect to the container is just the first option. Things get a little more complicated as soon as we have more than one Button, or in general any component, in the layout. If you click to place a second Button and then move its location around the screen, you will notice that now alignments are shown for the first Button as well as the parent container.

In a relative layout you can set the position of a component relative to the parent container or to any of the other components in the container. The Designer positions the component you are using relative to the nearest component or the parent container.

What this means is that if you position a second button relative to the first then the second button moves if you re-position the first. Try it to see how this works. The two buttons move together if you move the first button.

What is less obvious, but logical, is any relatively positioned components will move if the component they are positioned against is resized. For example, if a button is positioned relative to the right-hand side of another component then making the component wider moves the button to keep it aligned to the right-hand side.

As you might guess there are properties that you can use to position one component relative to another. For example layout_alignLeft and layout_alignTop set the alignment of the left and top of the control with the left and top of the specified control. Each of these properties is set by specifying the id of the control you want to align with. So, for example, setting layout_alignTop to @id/button aligns the top of the control with the top of the control with id button. Recall that @id/button is a reference to something defined in a resource file i.e. the id of the button.

This all sounds very complicated and it might leave you thinking that it is all unnecessary. However, it means you can build sets of components all aligned to one that is aligned to the container so that they all move together as a group. So you can place one component with an offset from another no matter what the size of the first component is. You can also set components to align with the left and right side of the screen and allow for rotation from portrait to landscape.

Despite all it is very easy to get into a complete mess with relative layout in the Designer. If components go missing then chances are they are on top of each other. The easiest way to sort this problem out is to go to the Properties window and manually reset one of the positioning properties.

It is helpful to notice the following:

- Use positioning relative to another component if it makes logical sense. That is, if you have a text entry component then it make sense to position its accept Button relative to its righthand side.

- If you position everything relative to the container parent then you effectively have an absolute layout.

- If the screen size changes then it is possible that components will overlap one another if there isn't enough space. Always make your layouts have plenty of unnecessary space.

- A good strategy when working with a group of components is to pick one that you position relative to the container then position all other components relative to it to ensure that you can move the group and keep alignments.

- Remember that some components can change their size as well as location and this can modify the position of components positioned relative to them.

It is also worth noting that there are other layout components and you are not restricted to the RelativeLayout component. The RelativeLayout component is used by default but you can change this for any of the other layout components - Constraint, Linear, Table, Grid and Frame.

One thing worth knowing at this early stage is that components have layout properties that are provided by their container so the set of properties that we have looked at in connection with the RelativeLayout component are unique to it. If you use another Layout then you have to learn about its layout properties from scratch. This is another topic we have to return to.

For most apps the RelativeLayout component is a good choice for a mix of Buttons, Text, Checkboxes and so on.

Sizing

In comparison to positioning sizing a component is almost trivial. All components have a Height and a Width property and these correspond to the drawn height and width when the component is actually rendered on the screen.

You may have noticed that there are what look like sizing handles on the components that you place in the Designer. However, if you try to drag these to change the size of, say, a button you will notice that often nothing much happens. For this reason sizing using the Designer can seem frustrating as it simply ignores your attempts to change the size of a control. The reason for this lack of responsiveness is that most components resize to accommodate their contents. This auto-sizing behavior is set by the layout_width and layout_height properties. You can override this by typing in an exact size, e.g. 100dp, into the value box next to the property.

You can also set a size in the RelativeLayout by aligning the right and left sides of a control or the top and bottom.

Also notice that you can set a maximum and a minimum size for most components.

Setting a maximum will result in the content being truncated if it doesn't fit. Setting a minimum is often the best plan because then the component will increase in size when necessary.

Gravity

Now we come to a property that needs to be discussed because it sounds important. Gravity is basically just another name for alignment. If you have a Button and you set its gravity property to Top then the text it contains will align to the top of the inside of the Button. There are a lot of alignment possibilities for gravity, but the majority are fairly obvious. The confusing part is that many components have a text alignment property which can be used to override the Gravity setting.

Gravity is particularly important when used with LinearLayout when the layout_gravity property sets how the component should align inside the layout, more of this in Chapter 6. Also notice that setting gravity on a component modifies how its contents display. This might not show in blueprint view.

The Component Tree

If you look to the bottom left corner of Android Studio in Design mode you will see a window called Component Tree. This is almost self explanatory and hardly needs explanation other than to draw your attention to it. Notice that you can see the tree structure of the layout starting at the Layout container. You can see that the default layout is RelativeLayout and you can see the all of the other components correctly nested within their parent containers:

Notice that you can select and delete layout elements directly in the tree. This is useful when you have a complex layout that has gone so wrong that you are finding it hard to select components reliably. You can also move elements around in the tree to change the way that they are nested.

A Simple Button Example

As a simple demonstration let's first place a Button on the Designer, aligning it with the parent container at the top left-hand corner as shown:

If you find it difficult to get a rough position and then enter the exact margins, remember that you can move to the Properties window and enter values directly:

The big problem with this approach is that if you later select the component and move it even a little the chances are it will snap to the edge and you will have to enter the property values again.

Next place a TextView on the Designer. In this case the alignment we want is for the text to be on the same line as the text in the Button. This is a baseline alignment, but if you have the Designer zoomed so that you can see the full area of the screen the chances are all you will be able to do is align to the top or bottom of the Button:

To achieve the baseline alignment you have to use a higher zoom so that you can position the TextView more accurately. Use the zoom tools at the top right of the Designer.

In many cases if you can't get the alignment you want then increasing the zoom to maximum is often the way to achieve what you are trying to do. In this case you can move the TextView near the correct location and it will snap to the baseline alignment:

You can see that the text baselines are aligned by the dotted line drawn under the text in the button and the TextView. Working at higher zooms means you can't see the entire layout and this makes things difficult.

So what should you do?

- You could buy a bigger monitor so that you can work interactively at 100% zoom all the time.

- You could undock the design window that that it has the full area of the screen to work with.

- You could use the fact that you know what you are doing to set the layout_alignBaseline to the id of the Button object using the property window.

In practice zooming in and out is usually the easiest option.

Orientation and Resolution

One of the biggest challenges in creating apps for Android is allowing for the range of screen sizes and orientations. Mobile app development is distinctly different from desktop development because of this need to deal with differing screen sizes. Even when your app is running on a fixed device, the user can still turn it though 90 degrees and change the screen dimensions in a moment and then turn it back again. So your app has to respond to these changes. Fortunately Android makes is easier for you by providing facilities that specifically deal with resolution and orientation changes, but you need to come to terms with this situation as early as possible in your progress to master Android programming.

Android Studio has lots of tools to help with the problem of variable layout. For example, it lets you see your layout in a range of devices, orientations and resolutions. This makes it so much easier.

We can test our layout in landscape mode simply by selecting the Landscape option:

The relative positions that you set in portrait mode are applied in landscape mode without modification and so it is important that you work on their specification so that the UI looks good in either orientation. If this isn't possible then you can provide a separate layout for each orientation.

You can also see what your UI looks like on the range of supported screen sizes by selecting from the list of devices that appears when you click on the **Device In Editor** button:

For simple layouts this is probably enough but Android has more up its sleeve to help you work with different sized screens. In particular you can make use of "fragments" and create a separate layout for each screen orientation and resolution. Fragments are advanced and the subject of a separate book, ***Android Programming: Mastering Fragments & Dialogs.*** On the other hand, using different layouts for each orientation and resolution is fundamental to Android UI design and you need to at least know it exists at this early stage.

The idea is quite simple - provide a layout resource for each orientation and resolution you want to support. The system will automatically select the resource layout needed when the app is run on a real device.

How this works is simple, but Android Studio has some helpful features that shield you from the underlying implementation. It is a good idea to first discover how it works and then move on to see how Android Studio does it for you.

If you create a new layout file called activity_main.xml, i.e. exactly the same name as the portrait layout file you have already created, but in the folder layout-land this will be used automatically when the user rotates the device into landscape mode. That is the layout file used in any situation is determined by the name of the folder it is stored in. With this new layout which applies only to a landscape orientation you can now create a layout that will only be used in this orientation.

What happens in general is that when your app starts the system picks the best available layout file for the screen according to what has been stored in the resource folders, i.e. layout for portrait and layout-land for landscape..

When the device is rotated the system restarts your app and loads the best available layout. If you only have a portrait layout then it is used for all orientations, but if you also have a landscape layout file then it will be used for landscape mode.

What has just been described is exactly what happens. To recap, there are folders for each resolution and orientation and you can create multiple versions of layout resources all with the same name. The system automatically picks the folder to use to load the layout appropriate to the hardware at runtime.

Android Studio, however, tries to present this to you in a simpler way. The project view hides the fact that different folders are used and simply shows you the different versions of the resource files with a qualifier appended - (land) for a landscape file etc.

Let's see how this works.

To add a landscape layout to the button and text layout given above simply use the **Create Landscape Variation** menu option.

If you can't find the Layout Variants icon as shown above you may have lost it because the designer window is too small – just resize it.

Initially the portrait layout is used as the template for the landscape layout. Make sure you are editing the content_main.xml file before you create the landscape layout based on it. This ensures that this is the file that is used as the template for the landscape version of the file.

The landscape version of the file will contain all of the UI components that the template file does. This means that your code can interact with it in the usual way without knowing that it is working with a different layout. All the code cares about is that there is a button or there is a textView - not where they are placed or what orientation is in use.

If you examine the Project window you will see the new layout file listed:

You can see that there are now two content_main.xml files and one has (land) added after its name. As already explained this is a simplification that Android Studio offers you.

If you switch to the Project Files view you will see that in fact the new layout resource is in a new directory, layout-land

Android Studio's view is simpler, but when you need to know where files are really stored this view is useful.

At first the new landscape layout is the same as the portrait layout, but you can edit it to make it more suitable for the orientation. For example, we might want to place the text under the button in landscape mode:

Now if you run the app using the simulator you will initially see the portrait screen, but if you rotate the simulator to landscape mode using the menu to the right, you will notice a pause where the portrait layout is visible and then it will change to the landscape layout.

If you view the app on a range of devices you can rotate to landscape and see your custom landscape layout.

In general the best plan is to create a complete portrait layout and generate a landscape layout as late as possible in the development so you don't have to repeat UI tweaks.

Also notice that the auto-switching of layouts causes a potential problem. When the layout is switched your app is restarted and this means that it can lose its current state. It is as if your app has just been started by the user. To solve this problem we need to look into the app lifecycle and discover how to preserve state, which is covered in Chapter 12.

You can also use the same approach to supporting different screen resolutions. The idea is the same - multiple layout xml files are provided one for each resolution and the system automatically picks which one to use. This is slightly more complicated than dealing with orientation because you might well have to provide different resolution images to make the layout look good. More on this after we have looked at resources and resource management.

This is just our first look at a particular aspect of app development that makes Android more complicated than developing for a fixed screen size and it turns out not to be so difficult as it might first appear.

A First App – Simple Calculator

As an example of building a simple app using RelativeLayout and the Designer, let's build a Calculator App. Some of the techniques used in this app are a little beyond what we have covered so far but you should be able to follow and it is time to show what something more than a single button app looks like.

This is a very simple calculator - all it does is form a running sum. It has just ten numeric buttons and a display. It takes the values on each of the buttons and adds them to a running total. There are no operator buttons, add, subtract or clear - but you could add them to extend its functionality.

Start a new Basic Activity project called iCalc or whatever you want to call it. Accept all of the defaults.

The principle of operation is that we are going to set up a grid of ten buttons. Set each button to 0 through 9 as a text label. We are then going to assign the same onClick handler to each of the buttons. All it is going to do is retrieve the text caption showing on the button, convert it to an integer, add it to the running sum and then store it back in the TextView after converting it back to a String.

Put simply, when a button is clicked the event handler is called which retrieves the button's label as a digit and adds it to the running total on display.

Code

So the code is fairly easy.

We need a private field to keep the running total in:

```
private int total = 0;
```

Next we need an onButtonClick function which is going to be used to handle the onClick event for all of the buttons. Refer back to Chapter 2 if you don't know about simple event handling.

The button that the user clicks is passed as a View object as the only argument to the function and we can use this to get its text caption:

```
public void onButtonClick(View v) {
 Button button = (Button) v;
 String bText = button.getText().toString();
```

Now that we have the button's caption, 0, 1, 2 and so on, we can convert it to an integer and add it to the running total:

```
int value = Integer.parseInt(bText);
total += value;
```

Finally we get the TextView using its id (see Chapter 2) and set its text to the total converted to a String:

```
TextView myTextView =(TextView) findViewById(R.id.textView);
myTextView.setText(Integer.toString(total));
}
```

The complete event handler is:

```
private int total = 0;
public void onButtonClick(View v) {
 Button button = (Button) v;
 String bText = button.getText().toString();
 int value = Integer.parseInt(bText);
 total += value;
 TextView myTextView = (TextView) findViewById(R.id.textView);
 myTextView.setText(Integer.toString(total));
}
```

Put this code within the MainActivity class as one of its methods, for example right at the end just before the final closing }.

When you enter this code you will see many of the classes and methods in red:

```
            return super.onOptionsItemSelected(item);

    private int total = 0;
    public void onButtonClick(View v) {
        Button button = (Button) v;
        ton.getText().toString();
[Cannot resolve symbol 'Button']   r.parseInt(bText);
        total += value;
        TextView myTextView = (TextView)
                findViewById(R.id.textView);
        myTextView.setText(Integer.toString(total));
    }
}
```

This is because they need to be imported to be used by the project. You can do this manually, adding the necessary import statements at the start of the file, but it is much easier to place the cursor into each one of the symbols in red and press Alt+Enter and select **Import Class** if necessary. This should be becoming second nature by now.

Notice that the error flagged in R.id.textView cannot be cleared - it is a real error. We haven't as yet defined the UI and textView doesn't exist. It will once we create the UI, so for the moment ignore the error.

Layout

Now we turn our attention to the layout. Open the layout file, delete the default text and place a single button on the design surface at the top right of the screen with a little space. We need to modify its text property and we can use a shortcut to get to it. If you double click on it you will be transferred to the text property window where you can enter 7 as its text property.

While in the Properties window and find the onClick property. Set this to onButtonClick, the event handler you have just written:

If you use the drop-down list of possible functions for the onClick event handler you might find that you have to edit out the (MainActivity) that Android Studio adds. If you leave it in then the app crashes as it is incorrectly included in the XML. The XML should read:

```
android:onClick="onButtonClick"
```

and not

```
android:onClick="onButtonClick (MainActivity)"
```

Be careful not to include any spaces or other characters or again it will not work. Also notice that the event handler is shown with (MainActivity) in the property window even if you have edited it out of the XML.

To create the grid of ten buttons select the first button and copy it to the clipboard. Next paste the copied "7" button to the design surface and each time position it within the grid relative to the buttons that are already present. If you can't find the new pasted button it is right on top of the button you copied.

Now you have grid of buttons that all say 7. Double click each one in turn and change the text to 8,9, 4,5,6, 1,2,3 and 0.

By using the copy and paste trick you now have ten buttons all set to the same onClick event handler and all you had to do was edit the Text property.

Try to make sure that each Button you add is positioned relative to one of the other Buttons. You can check that you have done this successfully by dragging the first, i.e. the 7, and see if they all follow! If one or two don't then try re-positioning them relative to one of the other Buttons. If you find any positioning difficult zoom in.

If you get into a mess delete them all and start over.

To make this look more like a keypad select the 0 key and size it so that it occupies a double width:

Finally add a TextView at the top. You can position it relative to the top row and the 7 key and then size it so that it spans the complete set of buttons.

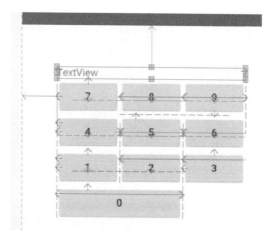

Now you should be able to move the entire block when you move just the 7 button to a new location. This doesn't always work because one or more of the Buttons is set relative to the container and you will find that the TextView has a tendency to snap back to its original size. It is good to know that you can undo an action by using Ctrl-z.

If you find the Designer too difficult to work with to create this layout, and it can be difficult, you might prefer to set the layout properties using the property window.

Finally run the program in the usual way and you will be please to discover your first app does actually calculate things!

Try rotating the emulator to see what it looks like in landscape mode.

Not bad but as promised as the app restarts you lose any calculation you were performing as the app is restarted when the orientation changes.

If you can, try it out on a real Android device. This lets you find out what it really feels like. Also do have a look at what the layout looks like on a range of screens and orientations.

This isn't much of a calculator, but you could make it into a really good one.

- Right align the text in the display
- Add a + and - button and implement the action
- Allow the user to enter multi-digit number
- Add a decimal point key and all a
  multi-digit float
- Add * an / keys
- Add a clear key

There are also better ways to implement the layout as you will discover in later chapters.

Summary

- You can create the XML layout file by hand, but using the Designer is easier.

- It is still useful to know how the XML file works so that you can edit it when the Designer lets you down in some way.

- The Designer modifies the way components look in the Layout mode by changing a component's properties.

- How you position a component depends on the Layout you are using.

- RelativeLayout lets you position components relative to each other or to the container.

- The Designer may change multiple properties to position the component where you want it.

- Use the Component Tree to select components that are difficult to select in the Designer.

- You can use the Property window to select and directly set any property.

- If you find positioning or sizing difficult in the Designer try zooming in.

- You can use Android Studio to view what your app looks like on various screen sizes and orientations.

- Different orientations and resolutions can be accommodated by creating additional layout files all with the same name. The system will pick which one to use at runtime.

- You can copy and paste components in the Designer to quickly build up repeated UI designs.

- A single event handler can be attached to many components.

Chapter 4

Android Events

Working with Android Studio makes building the UI easy with an interactive editor, but you still need to find out how to handle the things it isn't quite so good at. We now need to find out how to work with any event, not just onClick. Even though most controls can be used very successfully using just the onClick event - there are other types of event that cannot be handled simply by setting an onEvent property in the Property Window.

In this chapter we look in depth at Android event handling. As before, the emphasis will be on using Android Studio and the Designer to get as much of the work done as possible.

This is a moderately advanced topic and many Android programmers don't bother to understand events in their entirety preferring to just follow the boilerplate code given in examples. You can do this but understanding is usually better. Let's start with the problem of how to write an event handler in Java.

The General Android Event Handler

If you have used languages other than Java you might expect event handlers to simply be functions that are passed to UI controls to register them as event listeners, i.e. functions that are called when an event occurs. You might even have used an IDE that adds event handlers automatically for you. Android Studio currently doesn't do this - you have to add code to handle an event. It does, however, help with the automatic generation of this code.

Events in Java are slightly more complicated because you cannot pass a function as an argument like you can in JavaScript, C# and many other languages - you can in the latest version of Java, but it will be some time before UI frameworks and Android catch up.

Before Java 8 functions only exist as methods of objects so if you want to pass a function as a parameter you have to pass an object that has the function as a method.

As a result what has to be passed to register an event listener is more complicated in Java than in many other languages. The way that it all works was invented in the early Java UI frameworks such as GWT and later refined in Swing. Android uses the same approach.

As already mentioned you can't pass a function, you have to pass an object which contains a function that can handle the event. Clearly the event handling function has to be actually capable of handling the specific event and hence how it is defined, i.e. what parameters it accepts, depends on the type of the event.

For example an onClick event needs a handler that returns void and accepts a View object, which is the object the event occurred on.

To make sure that an event listener has the right sort of event handling event handling functions are defined using an interface.

An interface is like a class but it simply defines the functions that a class has to support. If a class inherits or implements an interface then you have to write code for each function defined in the interface. You can think of an interface as a specification for a list of functions you have to write to implement the interface.

The only things that are defined in an interface are the names of the functions and the types of the parameters they accept and return, for example the onClickListener is an interface that defines a single function

```
void onClick(View v)
```

Any class that implements the onClickListener interface has to have an onClick function of this type.

To create an event handler for the onClick event you have to do the following things:

1. Create a new class that implements the onClickListener interface
2. Define your custom onClick event handler within the class
3. Create an instance of the new class within the Activity
4. Use the button's setOnClickListener method to add the listener object created in step 3 to the event.

This is the general pattern that you have to follow when implementing any event handler. The only things that change are the interface you have to implement and the event handling function it defines.

The condensed way to remember all this is:

```
Event Class with event methods ->
 Event Object Instance ->
  Event Object set as Listener on UI component ->
   Event happens calls event method in Event Object
```

Sounds complicated - well it is and there are ways of simplifying it but first let's see how it is done exactly as described.

This is not necessarily the best way to do the job but it is how it all works in principle and it is important to understand what is going on.

Implementing An Event Handler Class

This is as much an exercise for Java beginners as it is an explanation of event handling. If your grasp of Java is good feel free to skip ahead.

Start a new project called FullClassEvent and add a button using the Designer. To implement an event handler for the onClick event first we need to add a new class to the project. Right click on the folder under the Java folder and select New, Java Class. A dialog box will appear. Enter the Name of the class as MyOnClickListener.   You can use the Interface(s) field to enter the name of any interfaces you want the class to implement. In this case we want it to implement OnClickListener and you can enter this with the help of a dropdown list that appears as you type. Start typing OnClickListener and select the View.OnClickListener interface line from the list as soon as it appears.

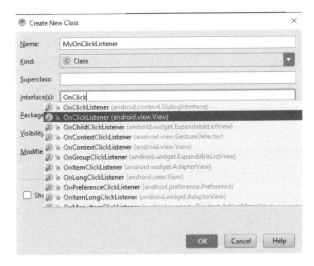

This creates the new Java file MyOnClickListener.java in the directory.

Note: For users of other languages it is worth pointing out again that Java has an almost unbreakable convention that each class is stored in its own file of the same name.

When you look at the new file in the editor you will see that it has some red underlining indicating that there is an error:

```
package com.example.mikejames.myapplication;
import android.view.View;

public class MyOnClickListener implements View.OnClickListener {
}
```

The reason for the error message is that you have to implement the methods defined in the OnClickListener interface. To indicate that you are going to implement an interface and then not do it is considered an error. The only alternative is to declare the class as abstract which means it doesn't define any methods and only exists to be inherited by other classes.

To get rid of the red underlining we have to define all of the methods in the interface. Fortunately Android Studio will do some of the job for us. Place the cursor on the line and type Alt+Enter to see suggestions for how to fix it:

Click Implement methods and select the methods you want to implement from the dialog box that appears.

In this case there is a single onClick method and Android Studio generates a method stub for you to fill in:

Next edit MyOnClickListener to read:

```
import android.view.View;
public class MyOnClickListener implements  View.OnClickListener {
 @Override
 public void onClick(View view) {
 }
}
```

Notice we have now created a class with a single method, which is our event handler. In a real case you would write lots of code in the event handler.

We have now completed the first step. Next we move to the Activity and place a Button on the design surface. At the end of the onCreate method we first retrieve the Button object:

```
Button button= (Button)findViewById(R.id.button);
```

Remember to use Alt+Enter to add any import statements that are needed. Next we create an instance of our event listener:

```
MyOnClickListener listener= new MyOnClickListener();
```

Finally we use the button's setOnClickEventListener method to connect its onClick event to our new listener object:

```
button.setOnClickListener(listener);
```

Putting it all together, minus some of the extra generated code:

```
@Override
protected void onCreate(Bundle savedInstanceState){
 super.onCreate(savedInstanceState);
 setContentView(R.layout.activity_main);
 Button  button=(Button)findViewById(R.id.button);
 MyOnClickListener listener=new MyOnClickListener();
 button.setOnClickListener(listener);
 . . .
}
```

Now if you run the program you will find that the onClick function in the MyOnClickListener instance is called when the button is clicked.

Using Breakpoints

The easiest way to check that the event handler is called is to insert a breakpoint on the first line of the onClick method. To place a breakpoint simply click in the "margin" next to the line of code. A red blob appears:

```
package com.example.mikejames.myapplication;
import android.view.View;

public class MyOnClickListener implements View.OnClickListener {
    @Override
    public void onClick(View view) {

    }
}
```

Now when you run the program using the Debug icon or the Run,Debug command the program will stop when it reaches any line of code with a breakpoint set. Once the program pauses you can see where it has reached in its execution and you can examine what is stored in all of the variables in use. You can also restart the program or step through it. There is much more to learn about debugging but for now it this small introduction is enough to save you a lot of time.

Other Events

The same overall method of creating a class that implements a method works for any type of event. You simply have to discover the name of the event listener interface, create a class that implements it, create an instance of the class and register the listener with the component that generates the event using a method something like setOn*Event*(*handler*). Notice that you register the event object i.e. listener, and not the event handler method i.e. not onClick().

This is a perfectly good method of implementing event handlers, but it isn't very practical because you are going to need to create a new class for every event you want to handle. In addition these classes are going to contain one method and be instantiated just once. This results in a lot of standard, "boilerplate" code for something that you are going to have to do often. There is also the problem of naming. You have to find a name for a class that is handling a click event from a button and another that handles the same event from a textbox and so on. You also need a name for each instance you create so you end up with lots of names like button1OnClickClass, button1OnClickObject and so on. There has to be a better way!

Now that you have seen the fundamentals of Java event handling we can explore two ways it tends to be done in practice.

Alternative Ways to Handle an Event

To avoid these overheads in creating event handlers you can use one of two possible methods:

- Implement the interface in the activity
- Use an anonymous class

The first is something of "clever fix" and it relies on the fact that any class including your Activity can implement an interface. The second is based on a language feature that was introduced into Java specifically to help with the need to create an instance of a class without having to actually create a class file or even give the class a name. Of the two the anonymous class is probably the better way to go about things, but you will see both used in other people's code and code examples so you need to know about both.

There is a third way of implementing event handlers that was introduced in Java 8 - the lambda expression. You can make use of this in Android Studio 2, but at the time of writing it involves changing the compiler in use and losing the advantages of instant run.

Implement the Interface in the Activity

One, almost cheat's way, of doing things is to simply use the MainActivity class to implement the event listener interface. After all, you can specify any class as an event handler as long as it implements the correct interface. It doesn't matter to the event mechanism that the class also implements lots of other methods that have nothing to do with events. This seems a little strange when you first see it but it is the closest approach to the way other languages do the job. For example, to handle the onClick event we need to add the "implements" for the interface to the Activity:

```
public class MainActivity extends AppCompatActivity
    implements View.OnClickListener {
```

Now all that has to happen is that the Activity class has to implement the onClick event handler. Don't worry about the fact that the line has a red underlining indicating an error - the error is that you have to implement the method. To do this place the cursor in implements and use Alt+Enter to display a menu of options that includes Implement methods:

If you select this you can select the methods you want to implement and Android Studio will add them to your code. In this case we just want to implement onClick:

```
@Override
public void onClick(View view) {
 //Handle Event
}
```

All that remains is to add the event listener using setOnClickEventListener. But what is the instance of the class that is providing the event handler? If you recall, what happens is that the system creates an instance of the MainActivity class to get your app running and the current instance of a class is always "this". So we need to add to the onCreate method:

```
button.setOnClickListener(this);
```

In many ways this way of doing things is the simplest. It has the disadvantage that you have to add an "implements" for each event you are going to handle, but this could be an advantage in that it enables you to see what events are being used in your Activity. Also notice that using this method you can set all of the event handlers using an instruction like:

```
somecontrol.setOnSomeEvent(this);
```

which also implies that you will be using the same event handler for an event irrespective of which control generated the event.

That is you will write a single onClick function and this will be used for all of the controls that you use setOnClickEvent(this) on. To handle this situation your event handler has to start by finding out which control generated the event and then deal with it appropriately.

If you want to use multiple event handlers, one for each control, then you need to use the anonymous class approach.

Anonymous Classes

Java has anonymous classes for just the situation we are trying to solve. It lets you effectively create an object, i.e. an instance of a class, without having to explicitly create a class, so providing a direct method of creating the event object.

Instead of:

```
Event Class -> Event Object -> Set As Listener
```

we just go straight to:

```
Event Object -> Set As Listener
```

The only downside of using anonymous classes is that you can't create a second instance of the class. It works only as a shortcut way of creating one instance of an object.

You create an anonymous class by writing the same code you would need to create an instance of an existing class but you add {block of code} following it to define the new methods of the new class you are creating. The result is an instance of the new class. For example suppose you have a class called Hello that displays a hello world message and you want an object that does everything that Hello does but with the addition of a goodbye method. Normally you would create a Leave class that inherits from Hello and defines the new method and then create an instance of Leave. Instead you can write

```
Hello leave = new Hello(){
   goodbye(){
        display message;
   }
}
```

This create an instance of Hello that has all of the Hello methods plus the new goodbye method. Notice that leave is an object and not a class and you can call methods such as leave.goodbye() at once. You have avoided having to create a new class just to create one instance of it. If the class you are extending has a constructor that needs parameters simply call the constructor in the usual way and add the code that extends the class immediately after.

So to create an instance of an anonymous class based on an existing class you simply start off by creating a new instance of the class and then tag on, in curly braces, all the methods you want to add.

In the case of an event handler you can take an interface and implement it as if it was a class and create an instance in one go. This is just shorthand, syntactic sugar if you like, for what we did in the previous sections.

For example:

```
MyInterface instance=new MyInterface{
   functions which are needed to implement MyInterface
}
```

creates an instance of the implementation of MyInterface that is contained within the braces with no need to define a class to get an instance of it.

For our onClick event handler using an anonymous class makes things much easier because we don't need a separate file to hold the new class and in fact we don't even need the new class just:

```
View.OnClickListener Listener= new View.OnClickListener(){
 @Override
 public void onClick(View view) {
  //Implement event handling
 }
}
```

The instance of our custom listener, complete with our onClick event handler, is ready to be used as before:

```
button.setOnClickListener(Listener);
```

Of course, you can save the use of a variable and simply use the anonymous class in the setOnClickListener as in:

```
button.setOnClickListener(new View.OnClickListener() {
 @Override
 public void onClick(View view) {
  //Implement event handling
 }
});
```

We no longer have to use the Listener variable, but the cost is the need to remember to close the function call with a right parenthesis.

The really good news is that Android Studio will help you create the anonymous class. If you start to type in OnClickListener it will provide you with options to complete the name. When you select **OnClickListener** it will then generate dummy functions for all of the methods defined in the interface:

All you have to do is provide the code, in the body of each of the functions, that does what you want.

Code Folding

There is one small mystery that we have to deal with, even though it isn't really useful. Android Studio uses code folding to hide the details of blocks of code from you. Usually this is useful, but in the case of anonymous classes it can be confusing. For example if you type in the code above that sets the onClickListener then in folded view the code reads:

```
button.setOnClickListener{
            (view) → { //Implement event handling });
```

This is exactly how you would write the same code using a lambda, but you can't use lambdas in Java 7, which is what Android uses. So this way of representing the code is purely for looking at. If you click the small + button to the left you will see the code expand to reveal the full version.

If you could use lambdas in Android code this would be the best way to implement an event handler, but you can't and so it is annoying that Android Studio taunts you with this better way of writing an event handler. You will be able to write code this way in the future and you can write it this way now if you are prepared to do some reconfiguration and give up instant run.

My advice is to write event handlers in one of three traditional ways and wait for lambdas to come to Android Studio.

Which Approach Should You Use?

In practice, the anonymous class approach seems to be the best because, while it is a little more complicated, it is completely general.

Using the Activity to implement the interface fails when you need different event handlers linked to each control. That is, suppose you have three buttons then using anonymous classes you can set a different event handler to each button. If you implement the event handler in the Activity then the same event handler will be used for all three buttons and your code has to test to see which button has been clicked.

Of course anonymous classes have the opposite problem to implementing the interface in the Activity. You can't reuse the event handler because there is only one instance of it. That is, if you want three different event handlers, one for each button, you have to write out the code three times to create three instances.

The anonymous class approach makes a direct connection between the UI component and the event handling code you are creating. You only have to look at the setListener function call to see the code that handles the event. In this sense it is worth the extra effort and is the one used in the rest of this book. If you want to use the XML method introduced earlier for the onClick event, or implement the interface in the activity approach, then this should cause no problems.

Summary

- In Java you can't pass a function to set up an event handler you have to pass an object.
- Each type of event has its own interface which is use to create an object which has the methods needed for the event.
- The most direct way to create an event handler is to create a new class that implements the interface and then create an instance of the class to handle the event.
- To avoid the problems with having to create a new class for each event handler Java introduced the anonymous class. You can use an anonymous class to implement an event interface and create an instance of it in one move.
- Alternatively you can use Activity to implement the interface.
- At the moment you can't easily use lambda expressions to implement an event handler.

We have already used some UI controls in previous chapters, but now we have discovered how events work it is time to examine how they work and how you can change the way they look.

Basic Input Controls

The term control comes from the idea that the user "controls" your program using them. Widget or component are also terms that are used to mean the same thing. The Android community seems very sloppy about terminology.

The basic input controls are:

- Buttons
- Text Fields
- Checkboxes
- Radio Buttons
- Toggle Buttons
- Switches

If you have used other UI frameworks many of these will be known to you and you can probably skip to just the ones that interest you.

TextView also has to be included in the full list of basic controls, but unlike the Text Field it cannot be modified by the user, i.e. it is an output control only.

Starting right at the beginning, let's revisit the Button in a little more detail

Button Styles and Properties

There are two basic types of button, Button and ImageButton. The ImageButton is much the same as the Button but it has a src (source) property which can be set to an image which will be displayed as the button icon and it doesn't display any text.

The main properties that you work with in the case of a button are things like background, which can be set to a color or a graphic. You can spend a long time changing the way buttons look, but in the main the only important property of a button is its onClick handler. A button is in your UI to be clicked.

If you place a Button on the design surface you can use the Properties window to customize it. There are two distinct ways you can change the way a control looks. You can set a style or modify a property.

Setting the style modifies a set of properties to given standard values. You can set a style and then modify individual properties to tweak it. Often when you first start work on a UI you will set individual properties only later to formulate a coherent style to be applied to the entire UI.

Set the background of the Button to dark gray by clicking on the ellipsis at the right of the property:

The Resources window that appears gives you access to all of the resources that your program can make use of. Resources are a big part of programming in Android and we cover them in detail in later chapters.

You could enter a color for the background directly by specifying the value of RGB and optionally Alpha, its transparency. Using a resource, however, means that if you change the resource value in the future all of the UI components that make use of it change.

There are different types of resource you can select from and there are resources defined by the project, the Android system and any Themes you might be using. Sometimes you can't see these three categories because they are expanded into long lists.

In this case you want to select a color so select the Color tab and then the android list. Scroll down and you will see a set of predefined colors that you can use. Find background_dark and select it.

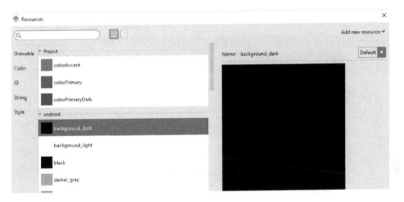

Of course, you now cannot see the text in the Button. To modify its color scroll down in the property window until you can see TextView. The Button is a composite object and it has a TextView object inside of it that displays the Button's text. If you drop down the textAppearance menu you will see textColor.

Simply select an alternative light color to use:

If you now place an ImageButton, located lower in the palette in Images & Media, on the design surface the Resources window opens at once. This is to allow you to select a "drawable", or icon, for the ImageButton to display. Scroll down until you find ic_menu_add. When you select it this becomes the src property for the button:

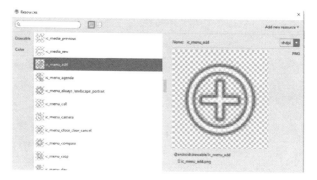

The result is these two buttons:

You can spend a great deal of time exploring ways to make use of a button's properties to style it just as you want it to look.

To attach a click event handler on both buttons you can simply define a function in the Activity and set the onClick property on each button to doButtonClick:

```
public void doButtonClick(View e){
 //process event
}
```

You can find examples of using buttons this way in earlier chapters.

Now that we know how to handle events using anonymous classes it is worth applying this, more sophisticated, technique. As we want to assign the same event handler to all three buttons we need to create an instance of OnClickListener. All you have to type is:

```
View.OnClickListener onClick=new O
```

and select OnClickListener when the suggestions appear after you type the O and let Android Studio generate:

```
View.OnClickListener myonClickListener= new View.OnClickListener() {
 @Override
 public void onClick(View v) {

 }
}
```

Notice it doesn't generate a final semicolon so remember to add it. You also need to fill in the details of the onClick event handler - there is only so much Android Studio can do by way of writing your program. Finally you need to set the instance on each of the buttons:

```
Button button =(Button)findViewById(R.id.button);
ImageButton imgbutton =(ImageButton)findViewById(R.id.imageButton);
button.setOnClickListener(myonClickListener);
imgbutton.setOnClickListener(myonClickListener);
```

Now when you click on either of the buttons the myonClickListener is called.

It is also worth noting that, while a button has no function in life other than to be clicked, all of the other controls can also respond to an onClick event. That is you can use anything as a button if you want to.

All Properties

If you have looked at any example of using Buttons in the documentation, or if you look at slightly older Android code, you may discover some properties that you can't seem to access using Android Studio. This is because the Properties window only shows you the most used properties. To see them all you need to click on the two arrow icon at the top or bottom of the window. The big problem with is is that you go from a very small subset to an overwhelming list.

The best way to deal with this is to know what you want to change and find the exact name of the property that does the job. This is easier to say than to do in many cases. For example, suppose you want to set an icon within a standard text button so that it displays to the left of the text that button contains. This appears to be impossible if you restrict yourself to the properties presented in the initial property window.

If you lookup the details of the properties that Button inherits you will find

- drawableLeft
- drawableRight
- drawableStart
- drawableEnd
- drawableBottom
- drawableTop

which are not in the property window list. These allow you to display a drawable, i.e. a graphic or icon, at the location specified relative to the text.

Once you know the name of the property you can find it in the list of all properties:

Click on the ellipsis button next to it and select a drawable of your choice to display the graphic to the left of the text:

Text Fields

Text Fields are the way you get the user to enter some text for you to process and as you can guess they form an important part of most UIs.

There are a lot of Text Fields provided in the Toolbox. but they all work in the same way differing only in the type of input they expect the user to type. In the course of developing apps you will encounter most of them sooner or later, but you really only need to know how to use one of them to understand how they all work.

If you have used another UI Framework then you will have encountered some form of the Text Field before but the Android control is slightly different in that it generally offers the user a customized virtual keyboard referred to as an IME (Input Method Editor). You can build your own IMEs, but for the moment let's just use the ones provided by the system.

If you want the Android emulator to make use of the IME that a real Android device would use then you need to deselect the Hardware Keyboard Present option when you are creating the AVD (Android Virtual Device). If the emulator makes use of the host machine's keyboard you don't see the IME at all.

The first thing to clear up is that even though there appear to be a lot of different types of Text Field controls in the Toolbox, they are all examples of the EditText control with its inputType property set to a particular value. When you place one on the design surface you will see that it is of type EditText and if you scroll down to its inputType property you can change the type of input the Text Field will handle.

When you use a particular inputType the user is presented with a virtual keyboard that is suitable for typing a value:

For example if you select a numeric type you will present the user with a simplified IME that only shows numeric keys:

You also get an action key at the bottom right of the keyboard that the user can press to complete the action - Send in the case of an SMS message, for example. To select the action button for a particular keyboard you will need to use the All Properties view and select a setting for the imeOptions property:

For example setting it to actionSend forces a Send button, the green paper dart button, to be displayed:

There are many other properties that you can use to customize a Text Field, but there is one standard task worth explaining in detail - writing a handler for the onEditorAction event.

The EditorAction Event

Returning to the EditText control let's add a handler for the Send button. This provides another opportunity for an example of the general process of adding an event handler.

First place an EditText for an email on the design surface and use the Properties window as described in the last section to add a Send button to the IME that pops up when the user enters text, that is find imeOptions and select actionSend.

Before you can handle any new event you have to discover the name of the event listener interface and the setOn method for that event. For the EditorAction event the listener interface is called OnEditorActionListener and the setOn method is setOnEditorActionListener.

With this information we can proceed as before and use an anonymous class to implement the event handler. In this case we might as well do the job within the setOnEditorActionListener as the event handler will only be needed by this one control:

```
EditText email = (EditText) findViewById(R.id.editText);
email.setOnEditorActionListener(
 new TextView.OnEditorActionListener() {
  @Override
  public boolean onEditorAction(TextView v,
                                int actionId,
                                KeyEvent event){

   return false;
  }
});
```

As before you don't have to type all of this in. Android Studio will generate much of it for you if you type **new OnEd** and select the correct option.

Now all that remains is to write the event handler, onEditorAction. You can lookup the details of the event handler in the documentation, but the generated stub for the handler function is often enough to let you know what the parameters are:

```
@Override
public boolean onEditorAction(
      TextView textView,
      int i,
      KeyEvent keyEvent)
```

In this case textView is the control that the event is associated with, i is the action id and keyEvent is null unless the enter key was used.

If the action has been "consumed", i.e. acted upon, then the routine should return true and no other handlers will get a chance to process it. In general, Java events can be passed on to other controls that contain the source of the event.

For a simple example let's add a TextView and transfer the text that the user enters when they select the send button. Imagine that the scenario is actually sending an email or sms.

All we have to do is cast the v parameter to an EditText and find the TextView that we added to the UI. Then we test to see if the user selected the send button or some other button and if they did we transfer the text:

```
public boolean onEditorAction(TextView v,
                              int actionId,
                              KeyEvent event) {
 EditText email=(EditText) v;
 TextView tv=(TextView) findViewById(R.id.textView);
 if(actionId== EditorInfo.IME_ACTION_SEND){
  tv.setText(email.getText());
 }
 return true;
}
```

Notice the use of the EditorInfo static class to obtain the integer id corresponding to the send action. The EditorInfo class has lots of useful constants and methods.

If you run the app you will discover that you can enter an email address into the EditText field with the help of the keyboard and when you press the Send button the address is transferred to the TextView.

Checkboxes

A Checkbox is a fairly obvious UI element. It displays a small label, controlled by the text property with or without a tick mark next to it. The user can select or deselect as many checkboxes as desired.

In most cases you don't bother to deal with the state of a Checkbox until the user presses some other control, usually a big button marked Done or similar. Then you can discover the state of each Checkbox by simply using the isChecked method which returns true or false.

For example, if you have a Checkbox with id checkBox then you can discover its state when a button somewhere on the view is clicked using:

```
public void onClick(View v){
 CheckBox box= (CheckBox) findViewById(R.id.checkBox);
 boolean checked = box.isChecked();
}
```

The Checkbox also supports the onClick event and this can be used to process changes to its state and you can setup the onClick event handler using the Properties window as in the case of a Button.

So to handle the checkBox change of state all you have to do is set its onClick event handler to:

```
public void onClick(View v){
 CheckBox box=(CheckBox) v;
 boolean checked = box.isChecked();
}
```

If you need to modify a CheckBox value then use the setChecked or the toggle methods.

Switches and Toggle buttons

Switches and Toggle buttons are just CheckBoxes in another format. They store one of two states and they change state when the user clicks on them, just like a CheckBox.

In Android Studio 2.2 a Toggle button causes an error when you place it on the design surface. You can still work with it, however.

You can check the state of a Switch/Toggle button using the isChecked method and you can use its onClick event to monitor when its state changes. The only real difference is that you can use the textOn and textOff to set what is displayed when the switch/toggle is on or off.

Radio Buttons

The final "simple" input control is the RadioButton. This works like a CheckBox in that it can be in one of two states, but the big difference is that a set of RadioButtons works in a group and only one of them can be selected at a time.

The reason for the term "radio button" is that, in the early days of electronics, car radios had mechanical tuning buttons arranged in a line which let the driver quickly select a station by pressing a button. When you pressed a new button the current button popped up so that only one button was pressed at any given moment, making sure that you only listened to one station at a time.

The only complication in using RadioButtons is making sure you group them together correctly. To do this we have to make use of a RadioGroup container which is used to hold all of the buttons that work together. There are a number of different containers used to group controls, but the most basic of these is the RadioGroup.

Using Android Studio you can create a group of RadioButtons by first placing a RadioGroup container on the design surface and then placing as many RadioButtons inside the container as you require. You will see the RadioGroup outlined in orange when you hover the cursor over it ready to drop a RadioButton into it. At the moment the Designer doesn't work very well with RadioButtons and it is better to simply drop each RadioButton into the top left of the RadioGroup and let the RadioGroup organize positioning. If a group of RadioButtons doesn't work as you expect, the chances are that not all the buttons are within the RadioGroup.

All the RadioButtons within a RadioGroup automatically work so that only one button can be selected at a time and you don't have to do any extra work to implement this behavior.

To find out which button is selected you can use the isChecked method as in the case of the CheckBox. In fact you can work with a set of RadioButtons in exactly the same way as a set of CheckBoxes, with the only differences being the use of the RadioGroup and only one button can be selected at any one time.

You can use the onClick event to detect when any button has been modified and the setChecked or the toggle methods to modify the state of a button.

Summary

- The basic controls that make up most of the simple Android UI are
- Buttons
  Text Fields
  Checkboxes
  Radio Buttons
  Toggle Buttons
  Switches
- Each control is customized using its properties and event handlers
- Some properties are hidden from you by Android Studio unless you select the All Properties button.

Chapter 6

Working With Layouts

The choice of Layout is vital to an Android UI. The Layout is what allows you to position and generally arrange other components. A good understanding of what is on offer in each of the available Layouts can make the difference between an easy and a difficult UI, from both the point of view of the programmer and the user. This is especially the case if you want to support a range of devices.

All of the classes and objects that make up the Android UI are derived from the same base class, the View. That is, a Button is a View and so are the Layout classes. However Layouts seem to behave in very different ways to the simple Button and this raises the question what exactly is a Layout?

Understanding Layouts

A Layout is a container for other View-derived objects. When the Layout is asked to render itself, it renders all of the View objects it contains and arranges them inside the area of the display it occupies.

The default Layout used by Android Studio is the RelativeLayout and we have already looked at using it in earlier chapters, but it is not the only Layout you can use with the Designer.

There are six currently supported Layouts:

- ConstraintLayout
- GridLayout
- FrameLayout
- LinearLayout
- RelativeLayout
- TableLayout

The ConstraintLayout is new in Android Studio 2.2 and is currently the recommended layout to use. In fact it was set as the default layout in early previews but RelativeLayout was restored as the default when Version 2.2 became generally available. The ConstraintLayout can be thought of as a development on the RelativeLayout. In principle, is can be used to create any layout that you can implement using a combination of the other layouts. It is claimed that ConstraintLayout based UIs are easier to construct and faster because they are "flat" i.e. do not use multiple layouts nested inside one another.

Among the original layouts RelativeLayout and LinearLayout are the most used, with FrameLayout coming a distant third. The final two, TableLayout and GridLayout, are suitable for specialized types of UI and in Android Studio 2.2 are more or less unsupported in the Designer and you have to work directly with their properties. For this reason, this chapter introduces the basic layouts in order of complexity - Frame, Linear and Relative – and then looks at the ConstraintLayout that in theory can do the work of the first three.

Before looking at these alternatives and how to work with them it is worth getting to grips with the basic ideas of layouts and the principles they share in common.

Layout Properties

Mostly you tend to think of the properties that are relevant to a control as belonging to the control, but a layout can do its job in many ways and requires the control to have lots of very specific properties to determine how it is positioned. In other words, the properties that a control needs to work with a layout depend on the layout chosen and this makes things difficult to organize.

The simplest but unworkable way of implementing this would be to insist that every control implemented every property used by every layout, even the ones not currently being used. This is clearly inefficient.

The solution to the problem actually used is that each layout defines a nested class derived from LayoutParams, that has all of the properties it needs the control to define. The control that is to be placed in side the layout creates an instance of the appropriate LayoutParams class and so varies the parameters it has access to depending on the layout container it finds itself in.

That is, instead of defining every possible property that any layout could want, a UI component that can be placed in a layout uses the appropriate LayoutParams class to "import" the properties it needs for the layout it finds itself in. This means that a control has two types of property - its own and those that it gets from LayoutParams.

Thus in the Designer and in the Properties window a control's properties are shown in two groups:

- Properties that belong to the object
- Properties that are required by the Layout object.

You can tell Layout properties because they are of the form layout_*name* in the XML file. You can see them in the Properties window in the Designer:

So in the screen dump the layout_margin properties are supplied by the RelativeLayout.LayoutParams object, but the Padding property is something that the Button supports. In other words, which layout_ properties you see depends on what sort of layout the control is, but the other properties belong to the control and are always listed. It is also worth knowing at this early stage that the Designer often presents a simplified set of layout properties which it then maps onto a larger and more confusing set of layout_ properties in the XML.

Width and Height

The exact set of Layout properties that you see depends on the Layout you use. However, there are two that all Layouts support:

- layout_width
- layout_height

You might think that the width and height of a control were properties that should belong to a control, but here things are more subtle. A control doesn't necessarily have a fixed size. It can, for example, ask the Layout to give it as much space as possible, in which case the Layout sets the size of the control. This is the reason why controls have layout_width and layout_height and not just width and height.

You can set these properties to any one of three possible values:

- a fixed size, e.g. 24px
- wrap_content, which sets the size so that it just fits the control's content without clipping
- match_parent, which lets the control become as big as the parent Layout can allow

If you use the mouse to drag the frame of a control in the Designer then what happens depends on the control and the Layout.

In most cases the default set by the Designer is wrap_content and it will ignore any attempts you make to interactively size a control. Indeed, in most cases trying to interactively resize a control doesn't change the layout_width or layout_height properties. However, depending on the Layout in use you might appear to change the size of the control due to the setting of other layout properties, more of this when we deal with particular Layout types.

The point is that the layout_width and layout_height are not necessarily the only properties that control the final displayed size of a control. One thing is fairly certain, if you want to set a fixed size for a control then you need to type the values into the Property window.

Units

If you are going to enter a fixed size or a location then we need to know how to do it. Android supports six units but only two, pixel-based units, are used routinely:

- px – pixel
- dp - density-independent pixel

The unit that it is most tempting to use when you first start creating an app is px, the pixel because you generally have one testing device in mind with a particular screen size and resolution. This is not a good idea if you want your app to look roughly the same as screen resolution changes. For this you need the density-independent unit, dp, because it adjusts for the screen resolution. If the device has a screen with 160 pixels per inch then 1dp is the same as 1px. If the number of pixels per inch changes then the dp to px ratio changes in the same ratio. For example, at 320 pixels per inch 1dp is the same as 2px.

- By using density-independent pixels you can keep controls the same size as the resolution changes.

Notice that this does not compensate for the screen size. If you keep the number of pixels fixed and double the resolution then the screen size halves. A control on the screen specified in px would then display at half its original size. A control specified in dp would display at its original size but take up twice the screen real-estate.

- Using dp protects you against screens changing their resolution, not their physical size.

If you specify sizes in dp then your layout will look the same on a 7-inch tablet, no matter what resolution it has.

As well as pixel-based measures there are also three real world units:

- mm - millimeters
- in - inches
- pt - points 1/72 of an inch

All three work in terms of the size of the screen and the number of pixels a control uses is related to the screen resolution. If the screen has 160 pixels per inch then 1/160 in=1 px and so on. Notice that once again these units protect you against resolution changes, but not changes to the actual screen size. Your button may be 1 inch across on all devices, but how much of the screen this uses up depends on the size of the screen the device has. The danger in using real world units is that you might well specify a fractional number of pixels and end up with an untidy looking display.

The final unit is also related to pixels but is tied to the user's font size preference:

- sp – scale-independent pixel

This works like the dp unit in that it is scaled with the device's resolution but it is also scaled by the users default font size preference. If the user sets a larger font size preference then all sp values are scaled up to match.

Which unit should you use? The simple answer is that you should use dp unless you have a good reason not to because this at least means that if you have tested your UI on a device of size x it should work reasonably on all devices of size x, no matter what the resolution.

Android Studio defaults to working in dp whenever you enter a value without a unit or when you interactively size or move a control.

A Control Is Just A Box

As far as a Layout is concerned a control is just a rectangle. Its size is given by layout_width and layout_height and these can be set by the control or, more often, by the Layout. Once the Layout knows the size of the control it can position it according to the rules you have established using the Layout's properties.

If you want to know the position that a control has been assigned then you can use its getTop and getLeft properties. This gives you the position of the top left-hand corner of the control's rectangle. You can work out where the other corners are using getWidth and getHeight, but to make things easier there is also getRight and getBottom. Notice that the position of the top left-hand corner of the rectangle is always relative to the Layout it is in. That is, the position is not an absolute screen position.

It is also worth knowing that controls also support padding, dead-space inside the control. This is space left between the outside edge and the content. In addition some, but not all, layouts support margins, dead-space outside a control that can be used to add space between controls.

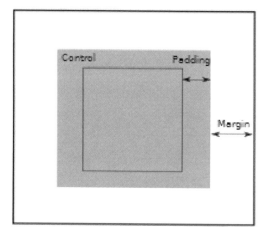

Notice that padding is a property of the control and margin is a layout property. You can set each margin or padding on the left, right, top or bottom individually or specify a single value to be used for all of them.

In theory padding is used to put space around the content of a control, but it can also be used simply to make the control bigger when its dimensions are set to wrap its contents. For example, the Button on the left has zero padding and the one on the right has a padding of 30dp all round.

Similarly margins are used to put space around a control, but they can be used to position one control relative to another or to its container. This is how the RelativeLayout works.

Gravity

Gravity is often regarded as mysterious, partly because of its name and partly because there are often two gravity properties in play. Basically gravity just sets where in a dynamic layout something is positioned.

Simple gravity settings are:

- top
- bottom
- left
- right
- center
- center_vertical
- center_horizontal

The meaning of all of these is obvious in that the object just moves to the specified position. However, things get a little complicated if you try to set an object to display at the left when the size of its container has been adjusted to fit, i.e. it is already as far to the left and the right as it can be. You can also set multiple gravity options. For example, you can set left and right at the same time and this just centers the object horizontally.

What makes gravity even more complicated is that there are settings that change the size of the object affected:

- fill
- fill_vertical
- fill_horizontal

In each case the object grows to fill the specified dimension.

There are also two clipping settings:

- clip_vertical
- clip_horizontal

These work with the top, bottom, left and right to clip an object to fit the container. For example, if you set gravity to top and clip_vertical then the object will be positioned at the top of the container and its bottom edge will be clipped.

Most of the time you will simply use gravity settings like center or top. If you try to use complicated combinations then things tend not to work as you might expect.

The final complication, which in fact turns out to be quite straightforward, is that controls have a gravity property and Layouts provide a layout_gravity property. The difference is very simple. The gravity property sets what happens to the contents of a control and the layout_gravity sets how the control is positioned in the Layout container. For example, if you have a Button and you set its gravity property to top then the text within the button will be moved to align with the top. If, on the other hand, you set the Button's layout_gravity to top the whole Button moves to the top of the Layout container. Notice that not all Layouts provide a layout_gravity property to their child controls.

The FrameLayout

The FrameLayout is the simplest of all the Layouts. It really doesn't do very much to position the controls it contains and is intended use is to host a single control, i.e. it really does just act as a frame around a control.

The Designer no longer provides as much help with FrameLayout as it did and if you have used an earlier version you may well find the new behavior frustrating.

hen you drop a control in a FrameLayout it is positioned at the top left and you cannot drag it to a new position within the layout. To set a control's position you have to find the layout_gravity property and set one or more of top, bottom, left, right, center_horizontal, center_vertical.

You can use this to position multiple controls in the same FrameLayout, but notice that if the total size changes the different controls may well overlap.

If two controls overlap in a FrameLayout, they are drawn in the order in which they were added. In other words, the last one added is drawn on top of the others. This aspect of the FrameLayout makes it useful if you want to display multiple controls and switch which one is visible. Simply put all the controls into the FrameLayout and select one to be visible using its visible property.

More commonly a FrameLayout is used simply as a placeholder for a component of a layout that isn't specified until some time later. For example, if you make use of a Fragment, see the companion book ***Android Programming: Mastering Fragments & Dialogs***, to create part of a UI or read in a list of things to display, then often you need a container for the new component to be present in your static layout. A FrameLayout does the job very efficiently.

- Use a FrameLayout when you need the simplest Layout that will hold one or a small number of components without the need for much in the way of positioning or sizing.

LinearLayout

The next layout we need to consider is the LinearLayout. This is a simple layout that can be used to do a great deal of the basic work of organizing a UI. In fact once you start using LinearLayout, it tends to be the one you think of using far too often.

In Android Studio LinearLayout occurs twice in the palette - once as a vertical and once as a horizontal LinearLayout. The difference, however, is just the setting of the orientation property to horizontal or vertical. In other words, you can swap a horizontal and vertical linear layout with a simple property change.

You can use a LinearLayout as the base Layout, replacing the default RelativeLayout that Android Studio provides, or you can place a LinearLayout within the RelativeLayout.

Android Studio really doesn't want you to use any Layout other than the RelativeLayout or ConstraintLayout as the initial container and so it doesn't let you delete the default layout. It will let you replace a RelativeLayout with a ConstraintLayout and vice versa, but you cannot delete or replace by any other layout. The reason is that replacing one layout by another is difficult because of all of the changes in the supported properties. You can edit the XML file directly to replace one layout by another, but you will have to re-edit all of the layout properties. You can replace an empty layout by another by editing the XML file and this is currently the only way to do the job.

The horizontal LinearLayout acts as a row container and a vertical LinearLayout acts as a column container. You can use nested LinearLayouts to build up something that looks like a table, but if this gets very complicated it is better to use a TableLayout. Nesting layouts like this is also inefficient at the rendering engine has to compute the layout multiple times to get it right. The advice is to use a ConstraintLayout and avoid nesting.

If you place a LinearLayout on the RelativeLayout then you can position it like any other control. If you then place other controls inside it then they will stack up horizontally to form a row or vertically to form a column.

This sounds easy but there are lots of ways to use a LinearLayout.

For example, if you put a horizontal and a vertical LinearLayout in the RelativeLayout then how they behave depends on what you set their layout_width and layout_height to. If you set it to wrap_content then the two Layouts act like a horizontal and vertical panel of controls, i.e. you can move all of the controls as a block.

It can be very difficult to be sure what you are dragging in the Designer as it is easy to pick up one of the Buttons rather than the layout. Make use of the Component Tree window to select the layout and to make sure that the Buttons are in the layout you think they are.

Things get more interesting when you nest one LinearLayout inside another to create a table. For example, you can create a calculator style keypad by nesting three horizontal LinearLayouts inside a single vertical LinearLayout. That is, place a vertical LinearLayout on the screen and then place three horizontal LinearLayouts within it. Within each horizontal LinearLayout place three buttons. If you have difficulty doing this use the Component Tree to make sure that the components are correctly nested. Make sure that you set the layout_width and layout_height to wrap_content, otherwise the LinearLayouts will overlap.

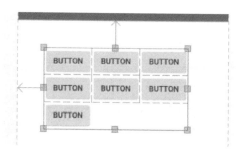

This is easier to arrange than using the RelativeLayout. The final Button is just placed into the vertical LinearLayout and it forms a row all of its own.

- LinearLayout is a useful grouping device whenever you need a row or column of controls.

Layout_weight

There's one last mystery of the LinearLayout to discuss, layout_weight, a layout property that only the LinearLayout supports. If you assign a layout_weight to any of the controls in a LinearLayout then the controls are adjusted in size to fill any unused space in proportion to their weights.

The really important part of this description is "unused space". What happens is that Android first computes the layout ignoring any weight assignments. This means that the controls are set to the sizes you specified. Next the system determines what space remains unused in the containing LinearLayout. This is then distributed between the controls that have non-zero values of layout_weight in proportion to their weights. For example, suppose we have a horizontal LinearLayout with three Buttons all set to wrap_content. The screen has been rotated to provide a lot of unused space for the example:

You can see that there is a lot of unused space over to the right. If we now set the first Button's layout_weight to 1 it will be allocated all of that unused space:

you now set the second Button's layout_weight to 1 then the unused space will be shared between the first two Buttons equally:

You can guess what would happen if we now set the third Button's layout_weight to 1, the space would be shared equally and all three buttons would be the same size. If, however, the first button was given a weight of 2 then the unused space would be shared out in the ratio 2:1:1 and so on.

More interestingly what do you think would happen if you assigned a fixed width to the third Button? The answer is simple.

If the third Button's layout_weight is zero then it is set to the width specified and the other two buttons get the unused space. For example setting the third Button to 350dp gives:

However, if the third button has a layout_weight set then it will probably change its width because it gets a share of the unused space just like the other buttons. In other words, when you set a non-zero layout_weight a control can change its size even though you have set a specific size for it. This leads to the idea of "measured size" and "actual size". In the case of the third Button its measured size is 350dp but if its layout_weight is non-zero then its actual size on the screen will be different - it will be allocated some of the unused space.

When you are working with components in code the getWidth and getHeight properties will give you the actual width and height of the control. The getMeasuredWidth and getMeasuredHeight properties will give you the measured width and height before any adjustment by the Layout has been performed.

Finally, it is worth pointing out that if you want to be sure that the three Buttons are the same size you have to set their widths to 0dp and weight to 1 (or the same value). Why is this necessary? When you set the widths to zero all of the space is unused and the system will divided it equally between each one. You can also set their widths to some constant minimum value and then let the weight mechanism share out the unused space.

RelativeLayout

The RelativeLayout has been used extensively in earlier chapters but now it is time to explain it in more detail. It was the one that was favored by Android Studio until the ConstraintLayout was introduced and it is still the default layout. It is a complex and sophisticated layout component and you might think that you should prefer simpler alternatives if at all possible. For example, you can often use a number of LinearLayouts to do the work of a single RelativeLayout. The most commonly quoted rule is that you should try to design your UI using the smallest number of Layouts. In particular, deep nesting of Layouts, i.e. one Layout inside another, slows things down because the system has to dig deep into each layer of Layout and this can take a lot of work. The rule is:

- Prefer a shallow sophisticated Layout to a deep nest of simpler ones.

You can usually replace a set of nested LinearLayouts with a RelativeLayout or a ConstraintLayout.

For such a capable Layout, RelativeLayout has only a few Layout properties. They fall into two groups:

- Properties concerned with positioning the control relative to the parent container
- Properties concerned with positioning relative to another control.

At least one of the controls in the Layout has to be positioned relative to the parent container to give the rest of the Layout a position. However, any number of controls can be positioned relative to the parent container if this fits in with what you are trying to achieve.

The RelativeLayout parameters are presented and organized by the Property window slightly differently to the way they are represented as constants in the XML or in code. This description applies to the way Android Studio presents them. Refer to the documentation for the XML or programmatic constants.

Edge Alignment

The principle is that you can specify the alignment of any pair of edges, one in the parent and one in the child. This will move the child control so that its edge lines up with the parent edge, for example, top edge to top edge. If you specify two pairs of edges then you can change the size of the control as well as positioning it. For example, top to top and bottom to bottom makes the child control the same height as the parent.

Layout Relative To Parent

The fundamental parent layout properties are:

- `layout_alignParentTop`
- `layout_alignParentLeft`
- `layout_alignParentBottom`
- `layout_alignParentRight`

which align the corresponding edge of the control with that of the parent container.

For example: setting layout_alignParentLeft moves the left side of the control to the left side of the parent.

This works without any resizing of the control. If you select two opposing alignments, top and bottom or left and right, then both the edges are moved and the control is resized. For example, setting layout_alignParentLeft and layout_alignParentRight produces:

You can also align to the center of the parent with:

- layout_centerInParent
- layout_centerVertical
- layout_centerHorizontal

Layout Relative To Another Component

The Designer used to map a confusing set of XML properties that positioned a component relative to another component. The latest version no longer performs this simplification. Instead you can either allow the Designer to work out how to set position relative to another component or you can work with the raw properties in the Properties window.

The basic idea behind all of the positioning properties relative to another component is that you simply supply the name of the other component to the relevant property:

- `layout_alignTop`
- `layout_alignLeft`
- `layout_alignBottom`
- `layout_alignRight`

For example:

`layout_alignRight= button1`

sets the right-hand edge of the control to align with the right-hand edge of button1. As always aligning two edges top/bottom and left/right changes the size of the control.

The properties:

- `layout_above`
- `layout_below`

align the bottom of the control with the top of the referenced control and the bottom with the top respectively.

Similarly the properties:

- `layout_toLeftOf`
- `layout_toRightOf`

align the left/right of the control with the right/left of the referenced control.

Finally the property:

- `baseline`

aligns the text baseline in the parent and child controls.

In API 17 a new feature was added to take account of the direction that text should flow within a layout, this caters for languages such as Arabic that start at the right-hand side and go towards the left. By default Layout_Direction is left-to-right and the start edge is the same as the left edge and the end edge is the same as the right edge. If Layout_Direction is set right-to-left then start is the same as right and end is the same as left. You can set startpadding to control the padding on the left or right depending on the layout direction set. All of the left/right properties have a start/end version.

Margin Offsets

So far all we can do is align pairs of edges.

How do you specify exact positions relative to another control or the parent?

The answer is to use the common pattern of setting the margins of the control. If you align top edges but set a top margin of 10dp on the child then the top of the child control will be 10dp lower than the parent control.

So the edge alignment is used to specify the relative direction of one control to another and the margins set give the exact offset.

RelativeLayout And The Designer

With all of this understood you can now see how the Designer lets you generate a RelativeLayout. As you move a control around the design surface the nearest other control or the parent Layout is selected as the parent to use for positioning, the closest edges are used for alignment and that margin is set to the distance between the parent and child.

This works well but it can sometimes be difficult to get the Designer to pick the control or the Layout as you move a control around. You can always use the Properties window to manually set this if it proves too difficult to set interactively.

Also notice that if you drag and edge of one control close to alignment with the edge of another control then this will result in just that edge being aligned and the control changes its size. For example if you drag the right side of a control to the right size of the Layout then the width of the control changes. This behavior can confuse beginners using the designer as it appears to be possible to resize controls by dragging an edge but most of the time the control snaps back to its original size when released. Of course it only resizes when the edge you are dragging lines up with a corresponding edge on another control.

It has to be said again that the Designer is not as easy to use with the RelativeLayout as in previous versions of Android Studio. For example it no longer supplies interactive positioning feedback in terms of pixel offsets and it no longer uses a simplified system of layout properties which map onto the real XML properties. These things might change in future versions.

Once you understand the way that the RelativeLayout works then using the Designer becomes much easier and so does using RelativeLayout to create a complex UI.

The ConstraintLayout

The ConstraintLayout is new in Android Studio 2.2 an it makes use of an additional library that is added when you select it in the palette. The support library is compatible with all versions of Android back to Gingerbread (2.3, API level 9) and so you can use the ConstraintLayout unless you plan targeting devices running earlier than Gingerbread.

ConstraintLayout was introduced in an effort to make layout more responsive to screen size changes and to improve the efficiency of layout by making it possible to avoid nesting layouts. It is, essentially, an improved RelativeLayout and if you have read the section on the RelativeLayout much of what follows will seem familiar. The Designer has been changed to work well with the ConstraintLayout at the cost of making the other Layouts harder to work with, presumably this will change as Android Studio continues to develop.

If you have an existing Layout then you can ask Android Studio to convert it to ConstraintLayout. All you have to do is right-click on the Layout in the Component Tree and select Convert to ConstraintLayout. This can be used to reduce a nested layout to a single "flat" ContstraintLayout, but be warned that in practice it often gets things very wrong. Often the best you can say of a converted layout is that it provides a starting point for reimplemenation.

Let's take a look at how the ConstraintLayout works in the Designer. If you drag a button onto the layout the Designer will give you information about alignments with other controls and the parent in much the same way that it does for the RelativeLayout.

Unlike the RelativeLayout, however, the Designer doesn't add any positioning to the control as you move it around. With the ConstraintLayout where you drop a component has no effect on where is will show when the app is run. In fact if you simply drop a UI component on the design surface without applying any constraints, when you run the app the component will drift up to the top left-hand corner. Notice that this means that where the component will appear in the running app isn't the same as where it appears to be positioned on the design surface and this can be confusing.

Using the ConstraintLayout the only thing that affects where a component displays are the constraints you apply. So how do you apply a constraint? There are two approaches, you can have the designer suggest them for you automatically or you can apply them manually.

Automatic Constraints

Automatic constraints are the easier to use and there are two ways to get the editor to apply constraints dynamically:

- Autoconnect mode – for a single component
- Infer constraints - for the entire layout

They do slightly different things and you need to learn to make them work together.

Autoconnect mode seems the more useful when you first meet it, but in practice it can be confusing and error prone. However, it is worth trying out. To turn Autoconnect on simply click its icon at the top of the Designer:

With Autoconnect on, when you place a component on the design surface the Designer works out suitable constraints based on where you dropped it, taking notice of how close it is to other components and to the edge of the screen. If the component it too far away from anything then no constraint is added. You have to use it to get a feel for how this works.

Once constraints have been added they are obeyed as you move the component around the screen. If the place that you first dropped the component wasn't suitable or if the constraints that were applied were inappropriate you might well find this a frustrating experience. Another frustration is that often the constraints aren't enough to determine the position of the control and then it drifts to the top left-hand corner. Also notice that Autoconnect only works when you first place a control on the design surface.

The Infer constraints option is actually easier to use but not as much fun to watch in action. All you have to do is position the components where you want them and then click the Infer constraints icon:

When you do this constraints will be calculated based on where each component is. This gives you more time to position the components and you can always delete all the constraints and click the Infer constraints icon again to recompute them. Only constraints that are necessary to fix the position of a component are added - existing constraint are not modified. This means you can use infer constraints to make sure that your layout has enough constraints to make it work - if none are added it was OK.

A good strategy is to switch off Autoconnect and use the infer constraints option every time you place a new component on the design surface. This allows you to build up a layout one component at a time and check each new set of constraints. You can then modify the newly added constraints and move on to the next component. Where things get difficult is when you have a multicomponent layout and need to make radical changes. Often it is easier in this case to delete all of the constraints and start again.

As long as suitable constraints are in place the ConstraintLayout works much like the RelativeLayout. For a component that has been placed on its own close to the top and left-hand edge of the screen, constraints will be added that fixes its distance from the left and top:

From now on when the button is displayed it will position itself at 80dp from the left and 80dp from the top. These constraints are applied no matter what the size of the physical screen is. It is worth knowing that the actual positioning is achieved, as in the case of the RelativeLayout, by setting the button's margin properties to 80dp. If you move the Button closer to the right-hand edge then it will not change to position relative to that edge of the parent, as is the case in the RelativeLayout. Once a constraint is set it stays set unless you delete it and apply a new one.

Just like a RelativeLayout, you can set constraints relative to the parent or relative to other controls in the layout. Try placing a second button on the surface and moving it close to the first. Now if you click the infer constraints button the constraints that are applied are taken relative to the first button:

You can see that in this case the second button is positioned 88 from the left edge of the first button and 32 below it. Once again these constraints will be obeyed no matter how large or small the physical screen the UI is displayed on. What is more if you move the first button the second button will keep its position relative to the first. This is exactly like the RelativeLayout and, as long as you set the correct constraints, anything you can do with RelativeLayout can be done with ConstraintLayout.

If you play with the positioning in the Designer you will quickly get the idea.

The big problem with the Designer automatically applying constraints is that it often gets it wrong. Working out how one control should be fixed relative to another really requires some intelligence and, at the moment, the Designer doesn't have it.

Manual Constraints

You can place constraints on positioning manually. All you have to do is drag a line from the constraint circles on the component to the edge you want to use as a reference point. For example, to position the button relative to the right side of the screen simply drag the circle on the right of the button to the right side of the screen and then move the button where you want it.

You can mix the automatic and manual setting of constraints and this is often the best way to work. In general you are specifying the constraint as the distance from some point on the component to a point on some other component. For example, if you want to place a component relative to another then simply drag the constraint point on the first to an edge of the second. In the case shown below manual constraints have been applied because constraint inference would have placed constraints on the left hand edge of the screen.

As well as being able to align different sides of a control, you can also set a baseline constraint so that text lines up. If you look at a Button in the Designer you will see that inside it there is a small elliptical box:

This represents the text in the Button and you can use it to setup a baseline constraint. All you have to do is select the TextView and hover the cursor over the elliptical box until it is highlighted and a message appears about dragging to create a baseline constraint - as shown above. Then drag from the

115

elliptical box to the baseline of the text in another component. This aligns the text in both components so that they share a baseline.

If you want to remove the baseline alignment then all you have to do is select the TextView, hover over the elliptical box and click when the message to remove baseline constraint appears.

So far the ConstraintLayout hasn't really provided anything new, but it does have a more sophisticated constraint that doesn't have a counterpart in the RelativeLayout. Referred to as "bias" this type of constraint works in terms of ratios, expressed either as fractions or percentages, and displayed as zig-zag lines. To use it you have to drag on two constraints. For example, if you drag one constraint to the left and its counterpart to the right the result is a horizontal bias used to position the control at the desired proportion of the layout size. You can achieve a vertical bias by dragging constraints from the top and the bottom.

As you drag the control around the screen the fractions or percentages are updated.

Alternatively you can use the sliders that appear in the Properties window to set them:

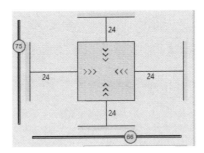

It is also worth knowing that the Properties window has a diagram that shows you the currently applied constraints and lets you modify them and set distances exactly:

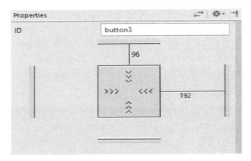

If you click on one of the constraint lines, you can enter a value for the distance. You can also click on the X that appears and delete the constraint completely. You can also set the default margin that is used for new controls.

Sizing

In comparison to positioning, sizing a component is almost trivial. You can see how the component is sized in the Properties window. The type of lines shown inside the component indicate the size of the component and its relation to its content. Straight lines indicate a fixed size:

An alternative to fixed size components is to allow them to automatically resize to fit or wrap their contents. To set this all you have to do is click on the inner straight lines which change to <<< and allow the component to change its size:

This auto-sizing behavior is set by the layout_width and layout_height properties. You can modify this by typing in an exact size, e.g. 100dp, into the value box next to the property.

Constraint Properties

As you might guess, there are properties very similar to those used by the RelativeLayout which set the constraints for a ConstraintLayout. To see all of the properties you have to click on the view all properties icon at the top right of the Properties window - the double arrow.

For example, if you look in the Properties window you will see:

`layout_constraintLeft_toLeftOf`

This prompts you to supply the id of the other control being used in the alignment – left-hand side to left-hand side in this case. There are similar constraints for the other possibilities. For example:

`layout_constrainBottom_toBottomOf`

and so on.

It is also worth understanding that, in allowing you to set the position of a component by simply dragging it to the location you want, the Designer is working out how to set multiple properties correctly. You could do this manually to get the same effect but the Designer does it simply from where you have positioned a component. This is why it is easier to let the Designer set the properties for you.

You can build sets of components all aligned to one key component that is aligned to the container so that they all move together as a group. It means you can place one component with an offset from another no matter what the size of the first component is. You can also set components to align with the left and right side of the screen and allow for rotation from portrait to landscape.

You can also set constraints which divide the available space up by percentages.

- The ConstraintLayout is fast and efficient compared to the alternative of putting one layout inside another. Unless you have a good reason it is the one to use.

Troubleshooting

RelativeLayout and ConstraintLayout provide a way of creating reactive layouts that adjust to the size of the screen. However doing this effectively is difficult. The amount of intelligence required goes well beyond what the constraint inference tool has. It may even be beyond a human. A simpler, but more work-intensive way, is to provide a separate layout for radically different screen sizes and use constraints to make small adjustments.

Given the advantage of producing a single layout that caters for a variety of screen sizes and orientations. it is worth persevering with, bearing in mind that it is very easy to get into a complete mess in the Designer. One very common problem is for components to apparently go missing. This is usually because they are on top of each other. The easiest way to sort this problem out is to go to the Properties window and manually reset one of the positioning properties.

You will also find the following tips useful:

- Use positioning relative to another component if it makes logical sense. That is if you have a text entry component then it make sense to position its accept Button relative to its right-hand side.

- If you position everything relative to the container parent then you effectively have an absolute layout.

- If the screen size changes then it is possible that components will overlap one another if there isn't enough space. Always make your layouts have plenty of unnecessary space.

- A good strategy when working with a group of components is to pick one that you position relative to the container then position all other components relative to it to ensure that you can move the group and keep alignments.

- Remember that some components can change their size as well as location and this can modify the position of components positioned relative to them.

Summary

- You can use different Layout containers to create UIs. Each Layout has its own facilities for how child controls are positioned and sized.

- The most important are FrameLayout, LinearLayout, RelativeLayout, and ConstraintLayout.

- Each Layout has its own set of layout properties to control positioning and sizing of a control. Child controls have an instance of the layout properties class to tell the Layout how to position and size them. All Layouts support layout_width and layout_height.

- You can specify position using a number of different units, but in most cases use dp (density-independent pixels) as this works the same way on screens of the same size but different resolutions.

- As far as the Layout is concerned, a control is just a rectangle, width by height, positioned using top and left.

- All controls have padding properties which specify extra space around the control's content.

- Some Layouts provide layout_margin properties that set extra space around the outside of the control.

- Gravity simply sets the simple positioning of an object - top, bottom, right, left. Every control has a gravity property which sets the position of its content, e.g. the text in a Button. Some Layouts have a layout_gravity property that sets how a control will be positioned.

- The FrameLayout is the simplest of all Layouts and just has layout_gravity for positioning. In most cases it holds a single control and it is most often used as a placeholder.

- The LinearLayout can be used to organize controls as a row or a column. As well as gravity, the LinearLayout also supports the specification of a control's weight. After the measured size of each control is determined by the Layout, the remaining unused space is allocated to the controls in the same proportions as their assigned weights.

- Complex layouts can be created by nesting LinearLayouts inside each other to produce a column or rows or a row or columns. This has resulted in the LinearLayout being the most used.

- The general principle is to try to select a Layout that results in the smallest nesting of Layout containers. It is therefore better to use a single RelativeLayout or ConstraintLayout rather than deeply nested LinearLayouts.

- The RelativeLayout can be used to create almost any UI, but it can seem complicated or difficult to use in the Designer because of the way properties are set and unset as you move controls around. The principle is that as you move a control the closest edge on it and on its parent container (or on another control) are set to be aligned and a margin property is set to the distance between them.

- You can resize controls using the Designer but only by dragging on an edge and aligning it with the same edge on another control. That is, you can make controls the same size but you cannot set a control to an arbitrary size.

- The ConstraintLayout is a further development on the RelativeLayout. It has tools that will apply constraints automatically for you but in practice the task needs some intelligence and manual constraints are nearly always better.

- The ConstraintLayout can be used to create all types of layout without the need to nest layout controls. This flat approach to layout is more efficient.

Chapter 7

Programming The UI

If you want to be a really good Android programmer, not only do you need to know how to create a UI, but also how the UI is created. To be really confident in what you are doing, you need to understand some of the inner workings of the Android graphics system. This is also essential if you want to modify the UI in code and work with menus.

A UI Library

There are lots of different UI construction kits for Java and other languages, AWT, Swing, Qt, MFC, WPF and on, and you might think that mastering them all would be a difficult, if not impossible, task. In fact it is a lot easier than you might think because most UI libraries use the same general approach and the Android UI library, which doesn't seem to have a given name, is no different. Let's take a careful look at how it works.

An Activity has a window associated with it and this is usually the entire graphics screen of the device it is running on. In other words, an Activity can allow other Java classes to draw on the device's screen. However, rather than simply providing direct access to the graphics hardware, there is an extensive set of classes that make building a UI and performing graphics operations easier.

Before we look at general graphics we need to first find out how the UI is constructed.

The View

The basis of all UI components and general 2D graphics is the View class. This is a general purpose class that has lots and lots of methods and properties that determine how it will display the component or other graphics entity it represents. It also takes part in the event handling system, which means Views can respond to events. There are View classes that implement all of the standard components that you make use of in the Android Studio designer, i.e. button, textview and so on.

Every View object has an onDraw method that can draw the graphic representation of what it represents onto a Canvas object which is essentially a bitmap with drawing methods. What happens is that the Activity calls the

View's onDraw method when it needs to update the UI and passes it a Canvas object that it then renders to the screen - you don't have to worry about how the Canvas is rendered to the screen at this level. You can think of this as, *"every View object knows how to draw itself"*.

To summarize:

- An Activity can be associated with a View object.
- When the Activity needs to draw its UI it calls the View objects's onDraw method e.g. view.onDraw(Canvas).
- The View object then draws on the Canvas whatever it needs to, whether a button, text or something else.
- The Activity then displays the Canvas object on the screen.

An Activity can only be associated with a single View object, which determines what is drawn on the screen. This might seem a bit limited but, as you will see, it is far from limited because View objects can be nested within one another.

Using setContentView

How do you set a View object to show in the Activities window?

The answer is that you use the Activities **setContentView** method, which is what we have been doing all along.

To see this in action, start a new Basic Activity project and change onCreate to read:

```
@Override
protected void onCreate(Bundle savedInstanceState) {
 super.onCreate(savedInstanceState);
 Button b = new Button(this);
 setContentView(b);
}
```

Don't forget to use Alt+Enter to add the import statements needed to allow you to use the Button class and don't leave any code in onCreate that would use other View objects such as the menu.

The first instruction creates a Button object, which is a subclass of View, and the second sets this as the Activities View. If you run this program what you will see is a gray area that fills the entire screen:

Yes, this is the button! You can even click it although, with no event handler, nothing happens.

To make this button a tiny bit more interesting we can customize it by setting properties. For example:

```
Button b = new Button(this);
b.setText("Hello Button");
setContentView(b);
```

If you run this you will see a button that fills the screen with the caption "Hello Button".

Don't bother setting any layout properties in code because at the moment there is no layout in force so they will be ignored. How to activate a layout is our next topic.

The ViewGroup

If an Activity can only show a single View object how can we ever create a complex UI with multiple buttons, textViews and other components? The answer, and you probably already guessed it, is that there are Layout, or ViewGroup, objects which can be used to host other View objects.

You already know about using Layouts in the Designer or in an XML file, but they, like all UI elements, correspond to particular Java classes that does the actual work.

A ViewGroup can display multiple View objects. So in nearly all cases the View object that is associated with an Activity is a Layout View. When the Activity asks the Layout View to render itself, by calling its onDraw method the Layout calls the onDraw method of each of the View objects it contains and puts them together to make a single result. Of course it also performs a layout operation positioning and sizing the View objects it contains.

So a Layout does two things:

- it hosts other View objects
- it performs the layout function after which it is named.

To see this in action try:

```
@Override
protected void onCreate(Bundle savedInstanceState) {
 super.onCreate(savedInstanceState);
 LinearLayout linLayout=new LinearLayout(this);
 Button b = new Button(this);
 b.setText("Hello Button");
 linLayout.addView(b);
 setContentView(linLayout);
}
```

If you run this program you will see a button right at the top left of the screen.

The first instruction creates a LinearLayout object. This is a subclass of View that can contain other View objects and it organizes them in a left to right or top to bottom way depending on the setting of its orientation property. Next we create a button object and then use the standard addView method of the LinearLayout to add it to the layout. All Layouts have an addView method and it can be used to add multiple View objects.

You can add more buttons to see how the default linear layout works:

```
protected void onCreate(Bundle savedInstanceState) {
 super.onCreate(savedInstanceState);

 LinearLayout linLayout=new LinearLayout(this);

 Button b1 = new Button(this);
 b1.setText("Hello Button 1");
 linLayout.addView(b1);

 Button b2 = new Button(this);
 b2.setText("Hello Button 2");
 linLayout.addView(b2);

 Button b3 = new Button(this);
 b3.setText("Hello Button 3");
 linLayout.addView(b3);

 setContentView(linLayout);
}
```

Programming Layout Properties

At the moment we are relying on default settings for the properties, and the layout properties in particular, of the View objects we are creating. However, in practice you could spend the time and lines of code to set all of the properties needed to create any user interface and layout you wanted to.

You now know how to create a UI completely in code. All you have to do is create all of the objects you need, set their properties and add them to suitable layout objects. This however is a little more complicated than you might think because each Layout type has a different set of layout properties. Exactly how this is done is easy enough, but if you don't want to know about it at this stage you can skip ahead as it doesn't change any of the general principles.

As explained in the previous chapter, each type of Layout has an associated class derived from LayoutParams called *layout*.LayoutParams where *layout* is the name of the Layout class. For example, LinearLayout has the LinearLayout.LayoutParams class, which is used to define all of the layout properties that a View object can use when added to a LinearLayout object.

You can probably guess how to make use of the LayoutParams class. All you do is create a correctly initialized instance of the appropriate LayoutParams class and use setLayoutParams on any View object you want to customize.

For example, to set the height and width in a LayoutParams object we could use:

```
LinearLayout.LayoutParams LP=new LinearLayout.LayoutParams(100,100);
```

There is a constructor for all of the LayoutParams classes that accepts just the width and the height properties. Once you have a LayoutParams object you can assign it to any View object by setting the View object's LayoutParams property:

```
b3.setLayoutParams(LP);
linLayout.addView(b3);
```

With this change the third button in our previous layout will be exactly 100 x 100 pixels.

Notice that the constructor works in pixels. i.e. px instead of dp (device-independent pixels). You can also use constants for MATCH_PARENT and WRAP_CONTENT. For example:

```
LinearLayout.LayoutParams LP=
        new LinearLayout.LayoutParams(WRAP_CONTENT,WRAP_CONTENT);
```

There is also a constructor that allows you to set the weight. Other layout properties have to be set using setProperty methods after the constructor has done its job. For example:

```
LP.setMargins(20,20,20,20);
```

which sets the left, top, right and bottom margins accordingly.

More complex Layout objects have correspondingly more complex LayoutParams that you have to spend time setting up.

So to be clear - there are properties such as Text that you set directly on the View object, but there are also Layout properties that you have to set on an appropriate LayoutParams object, which is then set as the View object's LayoutParam property.

The Layout Hierarchy

Notice also that a Layout can contain other Layouts and so the set of View objects that make up a UI is structured like a tree, the View hierarchy. When the screen is redrawn each View object is asked to draw itself and this is done for all View objects in the hierarchy from top to bottom.

Normally the View hierarchy is drawn just once when the Activity loads. If an area of the screen is obscured by another graphic for any reason, the redraw is clever enough not to draw the entire View hierarchy. It only redraws View objects that intersect with the invalidated area of the screen. The View hierarchy is also involved in passing events between objects and in determining which component has the current focus.

XML Layout

So far the principles of the graphic system are simple enough. Every control or component corresponds to a View object and you can build a UI by creating View objects in code and adding them to Layouts. You control the way the View objects are arranged using the LayoutParams object or by directly setting properties. An Activity will draw its View hierarchy to the screen when it needs to. OK, this is how to create a UI in code, but so far we have been building a UI using the Designer.

How does this relate to the View hierarchy?

The Designer creates an XML file which describes the View hierarchy that you want to create. The way that this works is fairly obvious. Each tag in the XML file corresponds to a View object of which you want to create an instance. For example:

```
<LinearLayout>
</LinearLayout>
```

creates an instance of a LinearLayout object.

Nesting tags within a layout indicates that the objects created need to be added to the layout as child Views. For example:

```
<LinearLayout>
 <Button />
</LinearLayout>
```

creates a LinearLayout object and a Button object and then adds the Button object to the LinearLayout using its addView method. You can see that the XML captures the idea of the View hierarchy perfectly.

To set object properties all you have to do is is use the corresponding attributes in the XML. For example to set the button's text:

```
<Button
  android:text="New Button"
/>
```

Layout parameters are set using properties prefixed with layout_property. For example:

```
<Button
 android:layout_width="wrap_content"
 android:layout_height="wrap_content"
/>
```

That is really all there is to it. The XML defines a hierarchy of objects and their properties and the system reads the file and creates the objects. This use of XML as an object instantiation system is not an uncommon one. Of course, the XML created by the designer looks a lot more complicated than the examples above, but this is mainly because of the number of attributes it defines. The basic idea is still the same.

Inflation Theory

The final big question to be answered is how does the XML get converted into a real object hierarchy? The answer to this is to use an "inflater".

To inflate a layout is Android jargon for instantiating the objects defined by an XML file. You normally don't have to call an inflater because the system does it for you behind the scenes, but you can if you want to. For example, to inflate a layout you would use an instance of the LayoutInflater. Normally you wouldn't create a fresh instance. Instead you can simply use an existing one supplied by the system using **getLayoutInflater**. Once you have the LayoutInflater you can use one of its many inflate methods to create a View object hierarchy as specified by the XML. Which method you use depends on where the XML is stored. You can simply supply a resource id for an XML file included in the res directory. For example to inflate the usual activity_main.xml layout you can use:

```
LayoutInflater inf = getLayoutInflater();
View myView = inf.inflate(R.layout.activity_main,null);
setContentView(myView);
```

The second parameter of inflate can be used to provide a View object to act as the root container for the inflated View hierarchy. The container is just used as a reference "parent" for the purposes of calculating the layout. That is, it simply provides the container that everything has to fit into according to the layout rules. Of course this is entirely equivalent to the usual:

```
setContentView(R.layout.activity_main);
```

which calls the LayoutInflater and sets the view in a single instruction.

The only reason that you would manually inflate an XML layout is if you wanted to do something clever, such as put one layout together with another or in some way manipulate the View hierarchy.

Notice that there are other types of inflater objects, e.g. the Menu inflater, which do the same job of converting XML to instantiated objects with the given properties. We will come back to these more specialized inflaters when we look at menus in the next chapter.

There is also a version of the inflate method:

```
inflate(R.layout.activity_main,root, true/false);
```

which will inflate the XML resource using root as its container for the purposes of layout if the last parameter is false and it will add the inflated View to the root if the last parameter is true.

Finding View objects

One problem we have to solve if you want to work with the View hierarchy created by an inflater is finding View objects in the hierarchy. In the example where we built the View hierarchy in code it was easy to keep track of a button or a textView by simply keeping a reference to when it was created.

An inflater simply returns the View hierarchy without an easy way to get at a particular object, a button say. One way of solving the problem would be to "walk" the View tree. A ViewGroup object, e.g. a layout, not only has an addView method but also a range of methods that allow you to access the objects it contains. Each child object is assigned an integer index - think of it like an array. The method:

```
getChildAt(i)
```

will return the child object at index i. You can also use:

```
getChildCount()
```

to find out how many child objects are stored in the container.

Using these methods you can search the hierarchy for the View object you want but how do you know which one it is? The answer is that all View objects have an id property which should identify them uniquely. There are getid and setid methods, but usually the id property is set as part of the XML file.

To avoid you having to work out an id value, the standard way of setting an id is to define a resource within the XML file:

```
<Button
    android:id="@+id/my_button"
```

When the XML file is inflated the @+ symbol is interpreted as "create a resource". An integer id is generated using the generateViewId method and this is used to both create the id property and to add a my_button property to the id property of the R object, R.id. The only minor complication is that when you set an id using the Designer it will auto generate the @+id/ for you. So in the Properties window you will see my_button not @+id/my_button. This is helpful but it can be confusing.

There is a lot more to say about resources, but for the moment this is enough to understand what is going on. Resources deserve a chapter all to themselves and you'll come to it after we've looked at menus.

What all this means is that not only do you get an autogenerated id value, but also a way to get this value into running code. You could use the getChildAt methods to step through all of the View objects in the hierarchy, but it is much easier to use:

```
findViewById(R.id.my_button);
```

which returns the object in one instruction.

The general method is to inflate the XML, set it as the content of the View and then use the findViewById to locate any View object you want to work with in code.

It is worth mentioning that a new way of working with View objects, data binding, is making its way into Android Studio. It will in the future make findViewById redundant and make the UI easier to work with. However it is important to know the basics of Android UI construction and for the moment it is better to use the tried and trusted methods.

How To Build A UI?

You now have two distinct approaches to building a UI. You can do the whole job in code or you can create an XML layout. In practice it is usually easier to use the Designer to generate the XML file for you. You can however mix the two approaches and change a UI "on the fly". For example you can load a UI by implicitly or explicitly inflating an XML file and then writing code to create and add other components or even remove View objects from the layout. To remove View objects you simply use the removeView or removeViewAt methods of the ViewGroup object.

There are other UI components such as menus that the Designer doesn't support. In this case you have to work with the XML or create the UI in code. This means you do need to know the inner workings of the View hierarchy even though the Designer is the easiest way to create a UI.

Summary

- All of the UI components are derived from the View class.

- An Activity can host and display a single instance of the View class set by one of its setContentView methods.

- You can create instances of View objects in code and set them to be displayed by the Activity.

- A Layout or ViewGroup object is a View object that can contain many View objects, so creating a sophisticated layouts that the Activity can display.

- Each Layout has its associated LayoutParams class, which is used by each View object it contains to control how it treats it within the layout.

- You generally have to create an instance of the LayoutParams class, set the parameters you want to determine and then set the instance as the LayoutParams of each View object that needs to use it via the setLayoutParams method.

- The use of Layout containers results in a View hierarchy, i.e. a hierarchy of View objects which are displayed by the Activity.

- You can also code the View hierarchy using XML. Each XML tag corresponds to a View object and they are nested to define the hierarchy. The properties of the objects are set within the XML as attributes. Layout properties are treated in the same way but with layout_ as a prefix.

- When the time comes for the View hierarchy to be assigned to the Activity, the XML file is converted into a nested set of View objects by the use of an inflater method. This simply reads the XML and converts each tag to an object and sets the objects properties.

- To find particular View objects in an inflated hierarchy the usual approach is to assign an id and use the findViewById method.

Chapter 8

Menus - Toolbar

A UI isn't just made up of buttons and other widgets or components, the menu is still a useful way of letting the user select what happens next. Android's menu system is easy to master. We also need to find out about the Toolbar implementation of the action bar.

There is a menu designer in Android Studio 2.2 but it doesn't work particularly well and in practice you have to work with the XML as text to create a menu. This presumably will change in later versions of Android Studio.

The basic principles of menu creation are the same as for building a UI in that a menu is a collection of View objects. You can create the View objects in code or you can use an XML file and a special inflater, a MenuInflater, to convert it into the objects. Defining a menu is more or less the same process every time, although the way in which you use the menu varies according to where and when the menu is shown, but even this follows roughly the same steps. Let's look a the general idea first.

Creating A Menu Resource

Menus are generally defined by a menu resource file, which is an XML file which is rendered to create the menu. All menu resources are stored in the app\res\menu directory. If you right click on this directory you can select the New, Menu resource option and type in a name - all lowercase as usual.

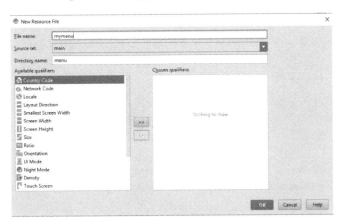

You can ignore the Available qualifiers for the moment. The idea is that each resource you create will be used in a given situation according to the qualifiers you select. In this way you can create custom menus for particular languages for example. More about this idea in chapter 10.

When you click the OK button the resource file is created and it will be opened in the layout editor. This in principle should allow you to edit the menu using drag-and-drop just like a general layout, but at the moment it is very limited and tends to create XML that doesn't work. You can place a menu item onto the menu and customize some of its properties, but this is about as far as it goes.

For the moment the best way to work is to select the Text tab at the bottom of the window and edit the XML directly. You will discover that it helps you enter the XML by suggesting autocompletions so you aren't entirely without help.

Before we can create a menu we need to know something about the XML tags we can use.

The Menu Tree

A menu is a hierarchy of options. The top level menu presents a set of items. If any of the items is itself a menu, i.e. a submenu, then it can contain more items.

Android menus make use of three objects, and hence three XML tags:

- `<menu>`
- `<item>`
- `<group>`

At the top level the <menu> tag inflates to a Menu object which is a container for menu items and group elements. The <item> tag inflates to a MenuItem object which is a single option in the menu. It can also contain a

<menu> tag which can in turn contain more <item> tags to create a submenu. The <group> tag doesn't inflate to an object. Instead it sets the group id of all of the items it contains. You can set various properties of a group of items in one operation i.e. they act as a group.

There are a range of attributes that can be used with <item> and <group> and not all can be used in every situation. The three that you need to know about are:

- id - an integer that you use to identify the menu item
- title - a string that determines what the menu item displays
- icon - a drawable image used when the menu item can be displayed as an icon.

With all this explained let's define a menu with a single File item and a submenu consisting of two items, New and Open.

```xml
<?xml version="1.0" encoding="utf-8"?>
<menu xmlns:android=
      "http://schemas.android.com/apk/res/android">
 <item
       android:id="@+id/file"
       android:title="File">

    <!-- "file" submenu -->
    <menu>
     <item
        android:id="@+id/create_new"
        android:title="New" />
     <item
        android:id="@+id/open"
        android:title="Open" />
    </menu>
 </item>
</menu>
```

You can see in the example that we have a top level menu item that we don't bother giving an id which contains a single <item> tag this displays the text File when the menu is displayed. In case you have forgotten the notation "@+id/*name*" automatically creates the id resource *name* and sets it to a newly generated integer value. You can then use *name* in code to find and work with the menu item.

The <item> tag contains another <menu> tag which in turn contains two more items that correspond to New and Open file menu options. You can see the structure in the Component Tree:

The Component Tree can also be used to do some limited editing of the menu by dragging-and-dropping to modify how items are nested.

Exactly how this simple menu looks depends on how it is displayed but it defines a menu with a single top level File option which when selected displays a submenu of two other options New and Open.

Displaying A Menu

There are four different ways you can display a menu:

1. Action bar such as the App bar
2. Context menu
3. Contextual action mode
4. Popup

The action bar or App bar was introduced in Android 3 as a replacement for the original options menu and has become the standard primary menu for apps and with Android 5 a new way of implementing it was introduced. The Toolbar is a standard widget that can be edited using the Designer. This makes it easier to integrate and work with. If you want to use the ActionBar in earlier versions of Android you need to make use of the Support Library - this is automatically included when Android Studio creates a project for you.

The context menu is a popup menu that appears in response to a long click on a component of the UI.

The contextual action mode is bar that appears at the top of the screen when the user long-clicks on a UI element and it is supposed to be used to provide actions that are appropriate for the item that has been selected. It too needs the Support Library to work with older versions of Android.

The popup menu can be displayed in response to almost any user action you care to use. It appears next to the View object that causes it to be displayed.

For example you could have a button that displays a popup when clicked or a popup could appear when a user types something into a text field. It is difficult to know exactly when to use a popup menu.

Logically the next step would be to use the XML file we just created to display either a contextual action mode or a popup, but as the default project type generates the code and menu resource file needed to implement an action bar, the Toolbar, and it is used in most applications, it is better to start with it.

The remaining menu types are the topic of the next chapter.

Using The Toolbar

If you start a new Basic Activity project called MenuSample then you will discover that it automatically creates a main_menu resource file and the code needed to display it as an App bar.

The Basic Activity template uses the support library to make it possible in earlier versions of Android. This is why the MainActivity class in your project has to derive from the AppCompatActivity class and not the more basic Activity class:

```
public class MainActivity extends AppCompatActivity {
```

and why we need the imports:

```
import android.support.v7.app.AppCompatActivity;
import android.support.v7.widget.Toolbar;
```

The Toolbar is defined in activity_main.xml as a custom widget:

```
<android.support.design.widget.AppBarLayout
 android:layout_width="match_parent"
 android:layout_height="wrap_content"
 android:theme="@style/AppTheme.AppBarOverlay">

 <android.support.v7.widget.Toolbar
  android:id="@+id/toolbar"
  android:layout_width="match_parent"
  android:layout_height="?attr/actionBarSize"
  android:background="?attr/colorPrimary"
  app:popupTheme="@style/AppTheme.PopupOverlay"
  style="@style/AppTheme" />

</android.support.design.widget.AppBarLayout>

<include layout="@layout/content_main" />
...
```

Notice that the Toolbar's style is set to AppTheme. This is important as the style selected changes the way the Toolbar is displayed and can stop it from displaying altogether.

Also notice the tag:

```
<include layout="@layout/content_main" />
```

This loads the layout that you design in content_main.xml. As explained in earlier chapters, the layout files are split into two parts - activity_main.xml which defines the layout that should be common to all Android apps and content_main.xml which is used for the layout specific to your app. The two files are automatically merged together when activity_main.xml is loaded.

When the Activity loads, onCreate runs and inflates the layout in activity_main.xml and the included content_main.xml. This is enough for the Toolbar to display, but for it to be used as a toolbar style menu by the system we need to add:

```
Toolbar toolbar =(Toolbar) findViewById(R.id.toolbar);
setSupportActionBar(toolbar);
```

All of this code is generated for you automatically and you will find it in the MainActivity.java file in onCreate:

```
@Override
protected void onCreate(Bundle savedInstanceState) {
 super.onCreate(savedInstanceState);
 setContentView(R.layout.activity_main);
 Toolbar toolbar = (Toolbar) findViewById(R.id.toolbar);
 setSupportActionBar(toolbar);
```

Now if you run the app you will see the familiar Hello world message and the default App bar:

In fact, this toolbar is so familiar you may not even have realized that it is a menu. It has the name of the app to the left and a three dot icon to the right.

If you select the three dot icon the Settings menu item appears:

If you take a look at the menu_main.xml file you can see the definition of this menu:

```
<menu xmlns:android="http://schemas.android.com/apk/res/android"
 xmlns:app="http://schemas.android.com/apk/res-auto"
 xmlns:tools="http://schemas.android.com/tools"
 tools:context="com.example.mikejames.myapplication.MainActivity">
<item
  android:id="@+id/action_settings"
  android:orderInCategory="100"
  android:title="Settings"
  app:showAsAction="never" />
</menu>
```

You can see that this defines a single menu with a single item with the title "Settings".

There are some new attributes being used in the item tag. The **showAsAction** attribute is important for the way the Toolbar, or action bar, works. By default the system places menu items into the overflow area that is only revealed when the user selects the three dot icon or more generally the action overflow icon. However, for items that you would like to give the user more direct access, you can set the showAsAction attribute.

This can be set to any of the following:

- **ifRoom** - show if there is room
- **never** - never show in the visible area
- **withText** - show with text
- **always** - always show even if it means overlapping other items
- **collapseActionView** - show a collapsed view of the item.

As you can see, the Settings item in the default Toolbar is set to never show.

The showAsAction attribute works with the orderInCategory attribute to determine the order in which items are shown.

To see this in action let's add another item, one to perform a Send, to the end of the menu_main.xml file before the final </menu> tag:

```
<item android:id="@+id/action_send"
 android:title="Send"
 app:showAsAction="ifRoom" />
```

Now if you run the app you will see:

The new Send item will be displayed as long as there is room. If there isn't it will appear when the user selects the three dots icon.

It is usual to show toolbar items as icons so change the item tag to read:

```
<item android:id="@+id/action_send"
 android:title="Send"
 app:showAsAction="ifRoom"
 android:icon="@android:drawable/ic_menu_send"/>
```

which specifies one of the many supplied icons:

You can carry on adding menu items to the Toolbar and customizing how they display given different screen widths. The general idea is the same for all menus.

Creating the App Bar

So far we have just looked at the menu_main.xml file and the XML specification of the action bar menu. There is also some code generated to actually create the menu displayed in the App bar. The Activity will fire a

CreateOptionsMenu event when it is ready to display the App bar - recall that before Android 3 there was an options menu rather than an action bar.

All the onCreateOptionsMenu event handler has to do is inflate the XML file that defines the menu:

```
@Override
public boolean onCreateOptionsMenu(Menu menu) {
 getMenuInflater().inflate(R.menu.menu_main, menu);
 return true;
}
```

The onCreateOptionsMenu is called once when the Activity starts. Before Android 3 it was called each time the menu was displayed on the screen, but now the App bar is always on display. How to change a Toolbar is discussed later.

All the event handler has to do is use the appropriate inflater object to create the menu from the resource file. The new View hierarchy of menu and item objects is added to the menu object passed to the event handler. This is important because it means that your new menu items are added to any that are already there. This allows other Activities and Fragments to add items to a common toolbar.

Where's My Toolbar?

If you try any of this out then there is a chance that you will do everything correctly and yet your Toolbar will not show.

There are only two common reasons for this.

1. You are targeting and using an early version of Android which doesn't support the action bar. This is unlikely especially if you are using the support library.

2. Much more common, is that you are using a theme that doesn't support the type of action bar you are using.

The solution is easy. For Android 5 or later, or when using the support library, select one of the AppCompat themes if you want to make use of the new features introduced with Android 5. As always, Android Studio generates the correct XML for the styles that work with the Toolbar.

Responding To Menu Events

You can attach click event handlers to the various items in a menu in the usual way. This is something that is often overlooked because there is a simpler and standard way of doing the job. However it is worth seeing the direct method if only to convince yourself that a menu is just another part of the View hierarchy that your application displays. If you aren't fully familiar with how to attach a click event handler to a View object refer back to Chapter 4 and 5.

When you inflate a menu resource in onCreateOptionsMenu what happens is that the View hierarchy that is created when you inflate the XML is added to the current menu. This is passed into the onCreateOptionMenu event handler in the menu parameter:

```
public boolean onCreateOptionsMenu(Menu menu)
```

Next you get the inflater and inflate the resource:

```
getMenuInflater().inflate(R.menu.menu_main, menu);
```

After this menu contains the View hierarchy, that is the entire menu as created so far.

If you want to attach an event handler to one of the menu items then you might think that the standard way of doing this is to use findViewById and then use its OnClickListener property to set the event handler, as you would with a set of View objects. You can't do this with the menu because it hasn't yet been added to the complete View hierarchy. The menu is only added to the View hierarchy after the onCreateOptionsMenu event handler finishes. That is the menu's View hierarchy is built up in menu and this is added to the apps full View hierarchy only when the onCreateOptionsMenu event handler finishes.

To allow you to find the menu item while in onCreateOptionsMenu, the menu object has its own findItem method. So to find the MenuItem that corresponds to the item with id action_send you would use:

```
MenuItem mItem=menu.findItem(R.id.action_send);
```

Now that you have the MenuItem object corresponding to the Send item you can add a click event handler:

```
mItem.setOnMenuItemClickListener(
 new MenuItem.OnMenuItemClickListener() {
  @Override
  public boolean onMenuItemClick(MenuItem item) {
   ....
    process event
   return false;
  }
});
```

Now the event handler will be called when the Send menu item is selected by the user. The event handler should return true if it has consumed the event and false if it wants to pass it on to other handlers.

The entire onCreateOptions Menu method is:

```java
public boolean onCreateOptionsMenu(Menu menu) {
 getMenuInflater().inflate(R.menu.menu_main, menu);
 MenuItem mItem=menu.findItem(R.id.action_send);
 mItem.setOnMenuItemClickListener(
 new MenuItem.OnMenuItemClickListener() {
  @Override
  public boolean onMenuItemClick(MenuItem item) {
   return false;
  }
 });
 return true;
}
```

You can also add an event handler for the menu in the XML resource using the android:onClick attribute. The event handler has to have the same signature as the one demonstrated above, i.e. it has to return a boolean and have a single MenuItem parameter. For example:

```java
public boolean myOnClick(MenuItem item){
 return true;
}
```

and:

```xml
<item android:id="@+id/action_send"
    android:title="Send"
    app:showAsAction="ifRoom"
    android:icon="@android:drawable/ic_menu_send"
    android:onClick="myOnClick"
/>
```

You can use this method to connect as many individual event handlers as you require for each of the MenuItems.

This is not the way it is usually done. It tends not to be a good idea to attach event handlers to the click events of each menu item. Instead the Activity has an onOptionsItemSelected event handler method which is called when any of the items in the menu is selected. Obviously this saves a great deal of effort because you just have to implement a single event handler - and you don't even have to hook it up to the menu.

Android Studio automatically generates an event handler ready for you to use;

```java
@Override
public boolean onOptionsItemSelected(MenuItem item) {
 int id = item.getItemId();
 if (id == R.id.action_settings) {
  return true;
 }
 return super.onOptionsItemSelected(item);
}
```

This just handles the single autogenerated Settings menu option, but you can see the general principle. The event handler is passed the menu item that has been selected - the actual object not just its id. You can then use the MenuItem's getItemId to retrieve the id and you can then test it against the ids that you assigned in the resource file.

So in our simple example with a Settings and a Send item we might rewrite the generated event handler as:

```
public boolean onOptionsItemSelected(MenuItem item) {
 switch (item.getItemId()) {
  case R.id.action_send:
    //perform send
   return true;
  case R.id.action_settings:
    //perform settings
   return true;
  default:
   return super.onOptionsItemSelected(item);
 }
}
```

You can see the general idea - test for each of the item's id in each of the case clauses and return true if you have processed the item event. This is the standard way of processing item events in menus, that is with a single event handler and a, possibly large, switch statement.

Changing Menus In Code

A menu is just a View hierarchy and so you can make changes to it just like any View hierarchy by adding and customizing View objects. However, menus have some extra considerations because they are displayed in a slightly different way to the rest of the UI. The problem is that the menu items are not always part of the View hierarchy. They are created when the menu is displayed. This means that you might try to modify them before they are present and so cause an application crash.

The key to modifying a menu on the fly is the **onPrepareOptionsMenu** event handler. This is called just before the menu is displayed and the menu View objects are included in the View hierarchy. The onCreateOptionsMenu event only fires once when the menu is created, but the onPrepareOptionsMenu is called every time the menu is redisplayed. Hence you can use it to make modifications to the menu.

Finding a simple example of its use is difficult as we will discover, so let's just add a new item via the onPrepareOptionsMenu. Select a suitable location in the class and right click, select Generate and then Override method. You can select onPrepareOptionsMenu from the list and Android Studio will create a stub for you:

```
@Override
public boolean onPrepareOptionsMenu(Menu menu) {
 return super.onPrepareOptionsMenu(menu);
}
```

Now all we have to do is use the add method to add a new item. There are a number of overloaded versions of add that allow you to specify the item in detail. The simplest is just add(CharSequence) which adds an item with the specified title:

```
@Override
public boolean onPrepareOptionsMenu(Menu menu) {
 menu.add("New Item");
 return super.onPrepareOptionsMenu(menu);
}
```

Now if you run the program you will discover that each time you select the Settings menu a couple of New Items are added to the menu.

What is going on? The answer is that each time the menu is drawn the onPrepareOptionsMenu is called. For example, if you cause the Settings menu to be displayed, this overwrites the menu display and hence it has to be redrawn and onPrepareOptionsMenu is called.

If you want to modify the menu in this way you need to check if it has already been made. In other words, you need to check the status of the menu to see if the item you want to add is already there.

A slightly more realistic example is to add and remove a menu item depending on the setting of a checkbox. Add a checkbox and change the method to read:

```
@Override
public boolean onPrepareOptionsMenu(Menu menu) {
 CheckBox cb=(CheckBox) findViewById(R.id.checkBox);
 if (cb.isChecked()) {
  menu.add(Menu.NONE,10,Menu.NONE, "New Item");
 }else{
  menu.removeItem(10);
 }
 return super.onPrepareOptionsMenu(menu);
}
```

Notice that all of the items added are given id 10 - there can be more than one menu item with the same id. If the checkbox isn't checked then the menu item with id 10 is removed. If there is no menu item with id 10 nothing happens and if there are more than one just the first is removed. Using this you can add multiple New Items and remove them by simply viewing the Settings menu which invalidates the menu display.

In a more realistic application you wouldn't wait for the menu to be invalidated by a user action. You would call invalidateOptionsMenu() when you wanted the onPrepareOptionsMenu to be called. So perhaps a better example is to add a button that calls onPrepareOptionsMenu to update the action bar:

```
public void onClickAddRemove(View v) {
 supportInvalidateOptionsMenu();
}
```

and have the onPrepareOptionsMenu only add the item if it isn't already in the menu:

```
@Override
public boolean onPrepareOptionsMenu(Menu menu) {
 CheckBox cb = (CheckBox) findViewById(R.id.checkBox);
 if (cb.isChecked()) {
  if(menu.findItem(10)==null){
   MenuItem menuItem = menu.add(Menu.NONE,10,Menu.NONE, "New Item");
  }
 } else {
  menu.removeItem(10);
 }
 return super.onPrepareOptionsMenu(menu);
}
```

Finally how do you set other properties of the MenuItem you have added? The answer is that add returns the MenuItem created. So to set the new item to show in the action bar you would use something like:

```
MenuItem menuItem=menu.add(Menu.NONE,10,Menu.NONE, "New Item");
menuItem.setShowAsAction(MenuItem.SHOW_AS_ACTION_ALWAYS);
```

Dynamically modifying the menu is a matter of keeping track of its current state and only then modifying it.

Controlling The Toolbar

There are a couple of questions that still remain. You can see how to add items, submenus and generally control what the Toolbar displays but what about controlling when it is displayed or how it looks? The answer to these question is based on working with the ActionBar object and as you might expect this is not something general to all menus. ActionBar has lots of features for showing menus in different ways and to cover it completely would take too much space. However it is worth knowing some of the basic customizations that you can apply.

You can get the ActionBar object in an Activity using getSupportActionBar or getActionBar. Once you have the ActionBar object you can use its show() and hide() methods to show/hide it as required:

```
ActionBar actionBar=getSupportActionBar();
actionBar.hide();
```

Similarly you can change the title and subtitle displayed in the action bar:

```
ActionBar actionBar=getSupportActionBar();
actionBar.setTitle("My Action Bar");
actionBar.setSubtitle("My Subtitle");
```

There are many other properties and methods that you can use to modify the way the action bar looks and behaves.

Things that are worth looking up are: using a split Toolbar; Up Navigation; Action Views; Collapsible Action Views; Action providers; and Navigation tabs.

Summary

- A menu is a hierarchy of View objects just like any UI element.

- You can create a menu in code, but using a menu XML resource file is the most common way of doing the job.

- There are Menu objects and tags which act as containers for Item objects and tags.

- Submenus can be created by nesting Menu objects within other Menu objects.

- Menu items can have a title, icon, and many other attributes which govern how they are displayed.

- There are four different ways you can display a menu: App bar/Toolbar; context menu; contextual action mode; popup.

- To make use of the App bar/toolbar and the contextual action mode in earlier versions of Android you need to use the AppCompatActivity and the other support classes.

- To display a Toolbar all you have to do is use the onOptionsCreate event handler to create a menu, usually by inflating a menu resource.

- In general you can handle click events on each menu item or, more usually, you can make use of an item's click event handler that the system provides that responds to a click on any of the items.

- For the Toolbar the item's click event handler is defined in the Activity as onOptionsItemSelected(MenuItem item)

Chapter 9

Menus - Context & Popup

As well as the all-purpose Toolbar which serves as an app's main menu, there are three other commonly encountered menus - the context menu, the contextual action menu, and the popup menu. They share the basic Android approach to menus while having some distinct characteristics.

The context menu is a floating menu that displays commands that take the item clicked as their subject. For example, selecting a line in a table might bring up a context menu that allows you to delete or move the item. The context menu is easy to understand and fairly easy to implement, however there is a slight confusion caused by the introduction of the Contextual Action mode, a context menu in the form of an action bar which is supported in Android 3 and above. A popup menu displays a list of items and is anchored to the View that invoked it. It can be used, for example, to provide additional choices to customize an action.

The Context Menu

Now that we have the principles of menu construction well understood it is easy to extend what you know about the action bar to other types of menu. To create a context menu is very easy once you know the basic mechanism.

You can register any View object in the UI to respond to a long click. When any registered View object receives a long click, the Activity's **onCreateContextMenu** event handler is called. This is where you create the menu that will be shown as the context menu.

Notice that you can register as many View objects as you like and each one will respond to a long click by onCreateContextMenu being called. This means that if you want to show a different menu for each View object you need to test to see which one has caused the event.

So the recipe is:

1. Create an XML menu resource
2. Register all of the View objects that you want to trigger the context menu using registerForContextMenu
3. Override the onCreateContextMenu event handler and use a menu inflater to create the menu

For a simple example create a new menu resource, right click in the res/menu directory and select new resource menu file option. Call it mycontext.xml and enter the following:

```xml
<?xml version="1.0" encoding="utf-8"?>
<menu xmlns:android="http://schemas.android.com/apk/res/android">
 <item
      android:title="MyItem1"
      android:id="@+id/myitem1" />
 <item
      android:title="MyItem2"
      android:id="@+id/myitem2"/>
</menu>
```

Next place a button and a checkbox on the UI and in the OnCreate method add the lines as shown below:

```java
@Override
protected void onCreate(Bundle savedInstanceState) {
 super.onCreate(savedInstanceState);
 setContentView(R.layout.activity_main);
 Button btn=(Button)findViewById(R.id.button);
 registerForContextMenu(btn);
 CheckBox cb=(CheckBox) findViewById(R.id.checkBox);
 registerForContextMenu(cb);
}
```

You can see what is happening here, We find the Button and CheckBox objects and register them using registerForContextMenu. After this a long click on either UI component will trigger the onCreateContextMenu event.

We need to add a handler for this event and we might as well let Android Studio generate the code for us. If you right-click at a suitable place in the Java code for the Activity and select the **Generate** and then the **Override Methods** options in the menu that appears you will see a list of methods you can override.

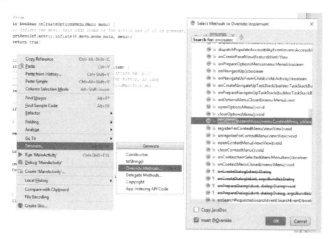

Select onCreateContextMenu and Android Studio will generate a stub for you. You can find the method you are looking for by typing in its name character by character and allowing Android Studio to show you matches in the list. Select the one you want as soon as you can see it.

All you have to do in this stub is inflate the menu resource file or otherwise create a menu object in code:

```
@Override
public void onCreateContextMenu(
        ContextMenu menu,
        View v,
        ContextMenu.ContextMenuInfo menuInfo) {
 super.onCreateContextMenu(menu, v, menuInfo);
 getMenuInflater().inflate(R.menu.mycontext,menu);
}
```

If you now run the program you will find that the same context menu appears when you long click on either the Button or the CheckBox.

Of course if you really want this to be a context menu then you need to test the View object passed into the onCreateContextMenu event handler and load the menu resource that corresponds to the appropriate menu for the View object. How do you handle the context menu item selection? In more or less the same way as for the Toolbar.

When any of the items in the context menu is selected the Activity's **onContextItemSelected** event handler is called. So all you have to do is override this and use the item's id to control what should happen. For example:

```
@Override
public boolean onContextItemSelected(MenuItem item) {
  switch (item.getItemId()) {
    case R.id.myitem1:
        do myitem1 action
        return true;
    case R.id.myitem2:
        do myitem2 action
        return true;
    default:
        return super.onContextItemSelected(item);
  }
}
```

The only extra detail is the availability of the **ContextMenuInfo** object which is passed to the onCreateConextMenu handler and can be retrieved from the item in the event handler using **item.getMenuInfo()**. This contains extra information such as which line in a list view has been long clicked. Exactly what information is included depends on the View object that generated the event.

If you want to see a context menu in action add a TextView to the UI and try:

```
@Override
public boolean onContextItemSelected(MenuItem item) {
 TextView tv= (TextView) findViewById(R.id.textView2);
 switch (item.getItemId()) {
  case R.id.myitem1:
   tv.setText("item1");
   return true;
  case R.id.myitem2:
   tv.setText("item2");
   return true;
  default:
   return super.onContextItemSelected(item);
 }
}
```

Contextual Action Mode

The context menu is easy to use but after Android 3 the Contextual Action mode menu is preferred as it extends the behavior of the action bar, taking over the App bar position at the top of the screen. However, it operates, and is implemented, independently of the App bar.

When a user long clicks a View object a contextual action bar appears at the top of the screen and not alongside the associated View object as the context menu does and it gives the user to opportunity to perform multiple actions. This may be the way to do things, but it is more complicated because it requires you to implement more code.

Contextual action mode can be used in earlier versions of Android via the support library which Android Studio automatically includes for you.

Unlike the context menu you don't just register UI components that trigger the menu. You have to call the startActionMode method to display the contextual action mode menu and this means you have to write a long click event handler. Notice that it is up to you what user action triggers the contextual action mode, but it is nearly always a long click.

The steps to creating a contextual action bar are:

1. First create an instance of ActionMode.Callback which contains methods for different stages in the menu's lifecycle.

2. You have to at least override the onCreateActionMode and this usually calls a menu inflater to generate the menu.

3. To handle events on the menu you also have to override onActionItemClicked.

4. To make the menu appear you have to call startSupportActionMode and pass it the instance of ActionMode.Callback you created earlier.

For example, if you have button and you want a long click event to trigger the menu you need to write in the Activity's OnCreate something like:

```
Button btn=(Button)findViewById(R.id.button);
btn.setOnLongClickListener(
    new View.OnLongClickListener() {
     @Override
     public boolean onLongClick(View v) {
      return false;
     }
    }
);
```

As before you can have Android Studio generate this stub by typing in the "new View.OnLongClickListener" and then right-click, select Generate and Implement Interface.

So far all we have implemented is an empty long click event handler for the button. To make the long click event display a menu we first need an instance of the ActionMode.Callback interface.

Again, you only need to enter the text up to "new ActionMode.Callback()" and then you can use the generate code option to implement the interface:

```
private ActionMode.Callback mActionModeCallback=
 new ActionMode.Callback(){
  @Override
  public boolean onCreateActionMode(ActionMode mode, Menu menu) {
   return false;
  }
  @Override
  public boolean onPrepareActionMode(ActionMode mode, Menu menu) {
   return false;
  }
  @Override
  public boolean onActionItemClicked(ActionMode mode,MenuItem item){
   return false;
  }
  @Override
  public void onDestroyActionMode(ActionMode mode) {}
 };
```

The Callback object has four methods each of which is called as part of the menu's life cycle. As you might well guess, to make the menu appear you have to fill in the details for the onCreateActionMode method:

```
@Override
public boolean onCreateActionMode(ActionMode mode, Menu menu) {
 mode.getMenuInflater().inflate(R.menu.mycontext, menu);
 return true;
}
```

All we do is inflate the menu resource and the system adds it to the menu. You can also fill out the details of the other methods - you most likely will want to add something onActionItemClicked, but this involves nothing new.

Finally we need to activate the contextual action menu in the button's onLongClick event handler:

```
@Override
public boolean onLongClick(View v){
 startSupportActionMode(mActionModeCallback);
 return true;
}
```

Now when you long click the button a new context action bar menu appears above the usual App bar:

Notice that this behaves a little differently in that the menu stays on the screen until the user clicks the right arrow button in the corner. You can allow the user to make multiple selections or dismiss the menu as soon as the user selects one option. In this sense the contextual action bar is more sophisticated and flexible than the simple context menu.

The complete code to make the contextual action bar appear is:

```
@Override
protected void onCreate(Bundle savedInstanceState) {
 super.onCreate(savedInstanceState);
 setContentView(R.layout.activity_main);
 Button btn=(Button)findViewById(R.id.button);
 btn.setOnLongClickListener(
  new View.OnLongClickListener() {
   @Override
   public boolean onLongClick(View v) {
    startSupportActionMode(mActionModeCallback);
    return true;
   }
 });

private ActionMode.Callback mActionModeCallback=
 new ActionMode.Callback(){
  @Override
  public boolean onCreateActionMode(ActionMode mode, Menu menu){
   mode.getMenuInflater().inflate(R.menu.mycontext, menu);
   return true;
  }

  @Override
  public boolean onPrepareActionMode(ActionMode mode, Menu menu){
   return false;
  }
```

```
@Override
public boolean onActionItemClicked(ActionMode mode,MenuItem item){
  return false;
}
@Override
public void onDestroyActionMode(ActionMode mode) {}
};
```

This introduction has just scratched the surface of how contextual mode menus can be used but the general principles follow the ideas of the general Android menu and many of the specifics of the action bar.

The Popup Menu

The final menu is so simple by comparison with the rest it is hardly necessary to explain how to implement it! What is more difficult is to say when it should be used. It certainly shouldn't be used as a substitute for a context menu where the operations affect the content that it is "attached" to. In the case of a popup it seems that its common use is to refine an action selection by providing parameters that modify it.

To show a popup menu all you have to do is instantiate a PopupMenu object, set its onMenuItemClick event handler, create the menu by inflating a resource file and finally using its show method. Where on the screen the PopupMenu shows depends on the View object you pass when creating the instance.

The steps are:

1. Create an instance of PopupMenu and pass the View object you want to use to position the menu.

2. If you want to handle item selection override the onMenuItemClick method.

3. Use the instance's inflate method to create the menu

4. Use the instance's show method to display the menu.

A popup menu is usually shown in response to some user action and so we need an event handler to create the popup in. If you place a button into the UI you can define its click event handler as:

```
Button button=(Button) findViewById(R.id.button);
button.setOnClickListener(
  new View.OnClickListener() {
      @Override
      public void onClick(View v) {
      PopupMenu popup=new PopupMenu(v.getContext(),v);
      popup.inflate(R.menu.mycontext);
      popup.show();
    }
});
```

The **onClickPopup** will be called when the button is clicked.

The PopupMenu constructor accepts the context and the View object it will be displayed next to. Usually this is the View object that the user clicked or interacted with i.e. the button in this case. Next we inflate the menu as usual but using the Popups own inflater which adds the menu to the Popup. Finally we call show which displays the Popup:

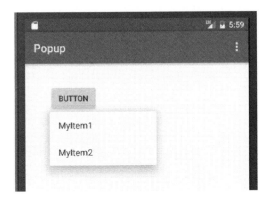

The menu is immediately dismissed if the user clicks on an item or on any other part of the display.

Of course if you were really using the popup menu you would also handle the item click event:

```
popup.setOnMenuItemClickListener(
    new PopupMenu.OnMenuItemClickListener() {
    @Override
    public boolean onMenuItemClick(MenuItem item) {
        TextView tv=(TextView) findViewById(R.id.textView2);
        tv.setText(item.getTitle());
        return false;
    }
});
```

Again you can get Android Studio to generate the stub using the Code,Generate command. As before you would use a select to discover which item the user had selected and act on that selection.

The complete code is:

```
Button button=(Button) findViewById(R.id.button);
button.setOnClickListener(
            new View.OnClickListener() {
 @Override
 public void onClick(View v) {
  PopupMenu popup=  new PopupMenu(v.getContext(),v);
  popup.inflate(R.menu.mycontext);
  popup.setOnMenuItemClickListener(
   new PopupMenu.OnMenuItemClickListener() {
    @Override
    public boolean onMenuItemClick(MenuItem item) {
    TextView tv=(TextView) findViewById(R.id.textView2);
    tv.setText(item.getTitle());
    return false;
   }
  });
  popup.show();
 }
});
```

Summary

- The context menu is invoked for all View objects in the UI that are registered using registerForContextMenu(View).

- When the user long clicks on any registered object the onCreateContextMenu and you can use this to display the menu. When the user selects any of the items in the menu the system the onContextItemSelected event handler is called.

- The contextual action mode menu is the most complicated to implement. You have to create an ActionMode.Callback object complete with methods to create the menu and handle events from its items.

- To display the menu you call the startSupportActionMode(Callback) specifying the Callback object to be used.

- If you want to use the contextual action mode menu on earlier versions of Android you have to use the support library classes.

- The popup menu is the easiest to implement. Simply create a Popup object, inflate the menu resource and use its show method to display the menu.

So far we have overlooked resources, but the subject can be ignored no longer. Resources serve too important a purpose in Android. They not only make localization easier, they are key to creating apps that adapt to the device they are being run on.

Why Use Resources?

Any small scale data that your app uses - strings, constants, graphics, layout files - should all be included as resources rather than hard coded into your app. For example, until now we have entered any text that the UI needed directly as a string property value. For a Button this approach has meant setting the Text property by typing in a string such as "Hello World".

Android Studio does it best to save you this effort. If you run the Warnings and Errors "linter" by clicking on the red icon in the Designer, then for any string you have entered as a literal into the Properties window you will see a warning:

While you shouldn't panic about every warning that the linter shows you, this one is a good idea because a resource can be reused in other parts of the program and it is easy to change without having to dive into the code. A much bigger advantage is that you can provide alternative resources, which are automatically selected by your app according to the conditions. For example, in this case you can provide strings in another language and they will be used automatically according to the locale in which the app runs. This is very a very powerful way to create custom apps that work anywhere in the world and on any device.

So how do we create a resource? It does depend on the type of the resource but in Android Studio there are two ways of creating a string resource.

The first is to click the "..." at the right of the property entry box which makes the Resources dialog popup:

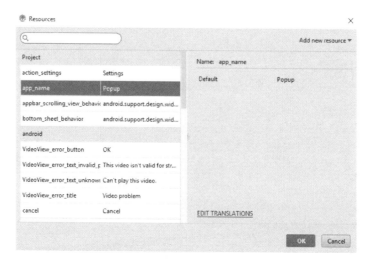

This lists existing resources defined by the system, the project and the theme in use. You can also use the Add New Resource dropdown to create additional resources. In this case a string resource:

All you have to do is enter a resource name and its value - the rest of the entries can be left at their defaults, their meaning will become clear as we proceed.

When you click OK you will see the Properties window with the entry:

`@string/Greeting`

This is a reference to your newly created resource. You will also see the string that you have specified appear as the button's caption. You can now reuse the string resource by entering @string/Greeting anywhere the "Hello World" string is required - of course it has to be used with a property that accepts a string. If you change the definition of a resource then obviously all of its uses are updated.

The second way of creating a string resource is to edit the resource XML file. If you look at the file strings.xml in the res/values directory you will find it contains:

```
<resources>
 <string name="app_name">Resources1</string>
 <string name="hello_world">Hello world</string>
 <string name="action_settings">Settings</string>
 <string name="Greeting">Hello World</string>
</resources>
```

You can see the hello world string that we have just added and some other strings that Android Studio creates automatically for you, including another hello world string which is used in the initially generated UI. You can edit the resource file directly or you can use the Resources dialog to create and edit existing string resources.

What Are Resources

- Resources are any data that your program wants to use.

Resources are compiled into your program's executable ready to be distributed to your end users as part of your app. For a string this doesn't seem particularly useful, after all you could just as easily use a string constant in code, but for other types of resource it can be the only way to get the data included in the app's executable.

For example, drawables, a range of different types of graphics objects, can be included as resources. If you include a .gif file as a resource then that .gif file is incorporated into your app by the compiler. This means you don't have to provide the gif as a separate file and you don't have to worry about where it is stored. Notice, however, that adding a .gif file to your app increases its size.

All resources are stored in folders within the res directory. The folder name gives the type of the resource and, as we shall see, can specify when the resource is to be used.

You can see a list of resource types in the documentation/ but the commonly used ones are:

- drawable/
  Any graphic - typically .png, .gif or .jpg but there are a range of other less frequently used type. The rule is - if its in any sense a graphic it belongs in drawable.

- layout/
  We have been using layouts since we started programming Android and XML layout is a resource complied into your app ready to be used.

- menu/
  The XML files that specify a menu are also resources and compiled into your app.

- values/
  XML files that define simple values such as strings, integers and so on. You can think of these as defining constants for your program to use. Although you can put any mixture of value-defining XML into a single file in the values/ directory, it is usual to group values by data type and or use.

  Typically:

  - arrays.xml for typed arrays
  - color.xml for color values
  - dimens.xml for dimensions
  - strings.xml for strings
  - styles.xml for styles

You can also include arbitrary files and arbitrary XML files in raw/ and xml/. There are two directories dealing with animation, animator/ and anim/. There is also a directory where you can store icons suitable for different screen resolutions, but more of this when we look at conditional resources.

Drawables

Drawables are slightly different from other resources in that there is no XML file that defines them. To create and use a drawable all you have to do is copy the graphic file that you want to use into the drawable/ directory. You don't need XML to define the resource because the resource's id is just the file name.

The best way to explain how drawable resources work is via a simple example. If you want to create a jpg bitmap resource all you have to do is copy the jpg file into the correct resource directory. Android Studio automatically creates the drawable/ directory for you and all you have to do is copy the bitmap file into it - but how?

The first thing to say is that the file name for a drawable resource can only contain lower case letters and digits. If the original file name doesn't conform to this pattern you can rename it after you have copied it into the directory.

There are two fairly easy ways:

1. You can find the file in the usual file directory structure and use copy and paste to paste it into the directory displayed in Android Studio.

2. Alternatively you can right click on the drawable folder in Android Studio and select Show in Explorer which opens the folder as a standard file system folder to which you can copy the bitmap file in any way that you like, drag-and-drop for instance.

Once you have the file, dsc0208.jpg in this case, in the drawable/ directory you can make use of it. Place an ImageView control on the UI using the Designer. The Resources window opens automatically for you select the drawable you want to use.

If you want to change the drawable at a later time find its src property in the Properties window and click on the ... button at the far right and the Resources window will open.

Select the Project tab and scroll down until you can see the name of the file you have just copied into the drawable folder and select it.

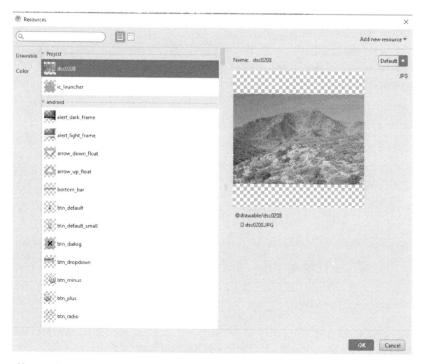

You will see that @drawable/dsc0208.jpg has been entered as the value of the src property - you could have entered this string directly without the help of the Resources window. You will also see the image displayed in the ImageView control:

That's almost all there is to drawable/ resources, but there is a bit more to learn about the different types of drawables that you can store there. This is best discussed when we cover graphics in general in the next chapter.

Values

The easiest of the resource folders to use is probably values/, but it also tends to be the least often used. The strings.xml file tends to be employed, but the others are underutilized. The reason for is is that the system tends to prompt you to enter strings as resources and there is an obvious advantage to string resources in that they allow easy localization. However, putting constants of all types in resources is a good idea.

Although the documentation only mentions string, arrays, colors, dimensions and styles, you can include a wider range of data types in the XML file:

- Bool

```
<bool name="resourcename">true</bool>
```

- Integer

```
<integer name="resourcename">1234</integer>
```

- String

```
<string name="resourcename">A String</string>
```

There are also two array types:

- Integer Array

```
<integer-array name="resourcename">
 <item>123</item>
 <item>456</item>
</integer-array>
```

- Typed Array

```
<array name="resourcename">
 <item>resource</item>
 <item>resource</item>
</array>
```

Dimension is also two easy-to-understand value resources:

- Dimension is simply an integer value complete with a units designator. For example:

```
<dimen name="resourcename">10px</dimen>
```

  Obviously you can use any of the standard Android measurement scales - pt, mm, in and so on. You use dimensions anywhere that you need to specify a size or location in a particular set of units.

Finally Color lets you organize the colors you are using in your app:

- Color provides easy to use names for hex color codes.

  For example;

  ```
  <color name="resourcename"> #f00 </color>
  ```

  defines a red color. You can specify a color using any of:
  ```
  #RGB, #ARGB, #RRGGBB or #AARRGGBB
  ```

  where each of the letters represents a single hex character with R= Red, G=Green, B=Blue and A=Alpha (transparency).

Ids

Ids are value resources and can be set up just like any other value resource. For example, if you want to set up an id for a button you might use:

```
<item type="id" name="resourcename" />
```

Notice that this is slightly different from other value resources in that you don't have to provide a value. The reason is that the system provides a unique integer value for each id. You don't often need to define an id in an XML file all of its own because ids can be created on the fly within other XML files. Putting a + in front of a resource id creates the resource without having to explicitly do the job. For example:

```
<Button
 android:text="@string/Greeting"
 android:id="+@id/button2"
```

creates the button2 resource.

On the other hand:

```
<Button
 android:text="@string/Greeting"
 android:id="@id/button2"
```

will only work if you have defined button2 in a resource file in the values/ folder.

Of course in Android Studio you can simply type in an id in the property window say and the system will automatically provide the +@id to make it auto-create. Note that sometimes there are problems if you delete an id using Android Studio because it leaves +@id, which isn't a valid id, in the XML. If this happens you have no choice but to directly edit the .xml file – which of course you now know how to do.

Accessing Resources In Code - The R Object

For much of the time you really don't need to bother with accessing resources in code because the job is done for you automatically. For example, if you assign a string resource to a button's text:

```
<Button
  android:text="@string/Greeting"
```

then the system retrieves the string resource and sets the button's text property to it when the layout is inflated. You don't have to do anything to make it all work. However, sometimes resources are needed within the code of an app and you have to explicitly retrieve them. You already have some experience of retrieving resources because you have used R.id to retrieve id values, but it is now time to find out exactly how this all works.

When your app is compiled by Android Studio it automatically creates a resource id, a unique integer, for every resource in your res/ directory. These are stored in a generated class called R - for Resources. The directory structure starting with res/ is used to generate properties for the R object that allows you to find the id that corresponds to any resource. This means that a resource id is always named something like R.*type.name*. For example:

```
R.string.Greeting
```

retrieves the resource id for the string resource with resource name "Greeting" that is:

```
<string name="Greeting">Hello World</string>
```

Notice that the resource id is an integer and not the string it identifies.

So how do you convert a resource id to the resource value?

The first thing to say is that you don't always have to. There are many methods that accept a resource id as a parameter and will access the resource on your behalf. It is usually important to distinguish when a method is happy with a resource id and when you have to pass it the actual resource value.

If you do have to pass the resource, or you want to work with the resource, then you have to make use of the Resources object. This has a range of **gettype(resource_id)** methods that you can use to access any resource. For example, to get the string with the resource name "Greeting" you would write:

```
Resources res= getResources();
String myString=res.getString(R.string.Greeting);
```

and myString would contain "Hello World". If you are not in the context of the activity you might have to use **Context.getResources**.

The only problem with using the Resources object is trying to work out which get methods you actually need.

There are also utility methods that will return any part or all of its resource name given the id:

- `getResourceEntryName(int resid)`

  Returns the entry name for a given resource identifier
- `getResourceName(int resid)`

  Returns the full name for a given resource identifier
- `getResourcePackageName(int resid)`

  Returns the package name for a given resource identifier
- `getResourceTypeName(int resid)`

  Returns the type name for a given resource identifier

There are also some methods that will process the resource as well as simply retrieve it. For example, if you have raw XML resource getXml(int id) returns an XmlResourceParser that lets you work through the XML retrieving tags, attributes, etc.

Conditional Resources

So far resources have just been a way to get data into your app. You might have thought that if there was another way to do the job then it might be just as good. However Android Resources are central to customizing your app so that it works with the wide range of device types and user that an Android app has to cope with. The clever part is that you can make use of conditional resources to provide a set of resources customized for the current device at runtime.

The idea is simple. First you provide a default resource file. This is the one that is located in the appropriate directory, /res/values say, but now you use qualifiers as part of the directory name.

For example you can create a directory called /res/values-es which is intended to provide resource values for the app when running on a device set to a Spanish language locale. What happens is that first any values that you have defined are taken from the XML files in the values directory, these are considered the default. Next if the app is running on a Spanish language device the XML files in values-es are processed and any resources with the same name replace the ones provided by the defaults.

You can see that this provides a fairly easy way to make sure that your app presents a UI in the local language, but there are more qualifiers than just locale and these allow you to customize the app for other features of the device. You can even stack up qualifiers as part of folder names to get more precise targeting. For example the directory values-es-small would only be used if the language was Spanish and the screen was similar to a low density QVGA screen. The only thing to be careful of is that the qualifiers are used in the order in which they are listed in the documentation.

There are qualifiers for locale, screen density, size and orientation, device type, night v day, touch screen type, keyboard availability and platform version (API level). You can find them all listed in the documentation but in most cases this is unnecessary because Android Studio helps you to create qualified resources.

If you select a resource directory, values say, and right click you will see New,Values resource file in the context menu. If you select this option then the New Resource File dialog opens. You can use this to create a resource file - just enter its name - and you can apply any qualifiers you want to by simply selecting from the list of available quantifiers to the left.

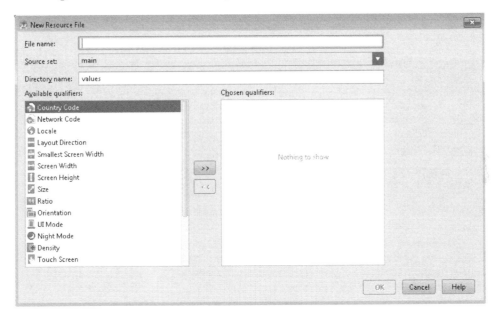

If you select Locale then you will be allowed to enter any details of the qualifier. In the case of Locale you can select the languages and regions you want to apply from a list:

Using the New Resource File dialog saves you a lot of time looking up qualifiers and language/region codes. It is much simpler than hand coding the directories and XML files. However you need to be aware of how Android Studio represents qualified resources to you in the project browser. For example, if you create a new strings file in the values directory and select Locale and es for the Spanish language in Any Region then this creates a directory res/value-es and a strings.xml file within it. So now you have

```
values/strings.xml
```

and

```
values-es/strings.xml
```

This is not what the project browser shows, however. It shows the new file as being in the values directory within another folder called strings.xml. The project browser is trying to show you the resource files with all of the similar files, i.e. strings, all grouped together in a single directory, but with qualifiers displayed to the right. In the case of locale it even shows the country flag as an icon.

This is a conceptual way of organizing things and it arguably makes working with multiple resource files easier. In this case you can see that the two strings.xml files are displayed as variations on strings.xml.

Working with Android Studio you can for the most part ignore the actual file and directory structure and simply add additional resource files using the New Resource File dialog, or for adding locales the Translation Editor described in the next section. Occasionally, however, you will need to find a file and manually edit the directory structure. In particular, there are no commands that allow you to modify the qualifiers associated with a resource file. The simplest solution is to delete the file and re-create it with new qualifiers if necessary. It is also worth mentioning that you can create custom layout files in the same way and that the Designer also has facilities to allow you to clone an existing portrait layout as a landscape layout, for example.

A Simple Localization

As we have already created a Spanish strings.xml file it is trivial to provide a Spanish version of the greetings string. All you have to do is edit the Spanish strings.xml to read:

```
<?xml version="1.0" encoding="utf-8"?>
<resources>
 <string name="Greeting">Hola Mundo</string>
</resources>
```

Now all you have to do is run the app and change the locale of the emulator or the real Android device. The simplest way to change the locale is to use the Custom Locale app:

When you run this you can see the current locale and select a new one:

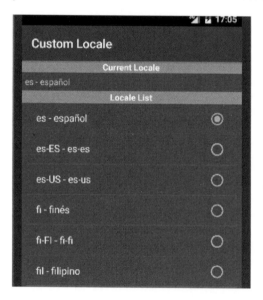

When you run the app in the emulator you will see the string resource retrieved from the Spanish strings.xml file:

Notice that while the button's text has changed the default strings.xml has been used for the other strings in the app.

It is very important to make sure that all of the resources you use have a default value. If you miss a resource out of a locale file that doesn't have a default you app will not run.

Android Studio Translation Tools

Android Studio also has some additional tools to allow you to preview conditional resources. The World icon and the Android icon that are displayed in the Designer allow you to select a locale and an Android version. It is worth using these to check that your app looks good in other locales.

If you are trying to maintain an app that supports a number of languages then the easiest way to maintain it is to use the Edit Translations option. This display an editor for string resources that shows each local version on the same line:

You can use this to enter translations of default strings and you can create new string resources across all of the locales with a single operation - enter the key, default and translations. You can also use the world icon at the top left to create new locales and this is by far the best way to do the job. There is even a link to order a translation from Google Translate.

Overall the Translation Editor is the best way to manage locales but occasionally you will still need to know how conditional resource files are organized, created and used.

Summary

- Use resources for as much data as you can. It makes it easier to change things.

- You can use the Property window to create and use resources or you can edit the XML directly.

- There is a wide range of resource types. In addition to layouts and menus, you are certain to use values and drawables.

- Drawables are an example of a resource that doesn't use an XML file. You simply copy the graphics resource files into the drawables directory.

- You can store simple data types in the values resource directory and this is often a better way to do things than using constants in the code.

- The R object is automatically generated and its structure mimics the resource directory structure. For each resource the R object has an integer resource id.

- Many methods take a resource's id and retrieve the resource for you. If you want to explicitly access a resource in code then use the methods that the Resources object provides.

- Conditional resources allow you to provide resources that suit the current device - locale, screen resolution and so on.

- Conditional resources work by applying qualifiers to the names of the directories that hold the resource files.

- Android Studio provides a simplified view of conditional resources that groups all variations on a resource file in the same organizational folder. This does not correspond to the file structure, but it is simpler.

- You can use the New, Resource File command to create conditional resources.

- The Designer lets you select which locale resource is used so that you can work directly with the localized layout.

- If you want to localize your app then make use of the Android Studio Translation Editor.

Chapter 11
Bitmap Graphics

Android graphics is a huge subject, but you have to start somewhere. In this chapter we look a simple 2D bitmap graphics, which is often all you need, and discover the basic principles of Android graphics.

Android Graphics

Graphics support in Android is extensive - from the simple display of images and 2D graphics through animation and on to full 3D rendering. To cover it all needs a separate book, and even then there would be topics left untouched. This chapter is an introduction to the minimum you need to know about 2D bitmap graphics in Android. It isn't all you need to know to get the job done, but it is enough to get you started on many common simple graphics tasks. With this grounding you'll also be in a position to seek out some of the additional information you need to do the less common things.

The key difference between this account of Android graphics and the typical approach you find in other documents is that it concentrates on the principles as well as the how-to. By the end of this chapter you should have a clear idea of what the different Android graphics classes are all about.

The Bitmap

You could say that the bitmap is the foundation of any use of Android graphics. The reason is that no matter how a graphic is specified or created, it is a bitmap that is eventually created and displayed on the screen.

There are many ways of creating or obtaining a bitmap. We have already seen how a bitmap file, .jpg, gif or .png can be included in the drawable/ resource directory and displayed in an ImageView control. In many cases a bitmap can be acquired by loading a file, reading in a collection of bytes or even taking a photo with the Android camera.

In this instance we will simply create a Bitmap directly:

```
Bitmap b = Bitmap.createBitmap(100, 100, Bitmap.Config.ARGB_8888);
```

A bitmap is simply a rectangle of pixels. Each pixel can be set to a given color but exactly what color depends on the type of the pixel. The first two parameters give the width and the height in pixels. The third parameter specifies the type of pixel you want to use. This is where things can get complicated. The specification ARGB_8888 means create a pixel with four channels ARGB - Alpha, Red, Green, Blue and allocate eight bits of storage to each channel. As four eights are 32 this is 32-bit graphics. The alpha channel lets you set an opacity.

There are many different pixel formats you can select and there is always a trade off between the resolution and the amount of space a bitmap occupies. However, ARGB_8888 is a very common choice.

Now you have a bitmap what can you do with it? The answer is quite a lot!

Most of the methods of the Bitmap object are concerned with things that change the entire image. For example:

```
b.eraseColor(Color.RED);
```

sets all of the pixels to the specified color, red in this case. Using the setPixel and getPixel methods you can access any pixel you want to and perform almost any graphics operation you care to. You can also work with the pixel data at the bit level.

The ImageView Control

How can you see a Bitmap that you have just created? The simple answer is to use an ImageView control. This isn't a popular approach however because it isn't as flexible as alternatives such as overriding the onDraw event handler. This said, the ImageView Control is very easy to use and sufficient for many tasks.

Start a new project and place an ImageView into the UI, accepting the defaults. As a demonstration of how you can use the ImageView to display a Bitmap change the onCreate event handler to read:

```
@Override
protected void onCreate(Bundle savedInstanceState) {
  super.onCreate(savedInstanceState);
  setContentView(R.layout.activity_main);

  Bitmap b = Bitmap.createBitmap(500, 500,  Bitmap.Config.ARGB_8888);
  b.eraseColor(Color.RED);
  ImageView imageview=(ImageView)  findViewById(R.id.imageView);
  imageview.setImageBitmap(b);
}
```

If you run the program you will see a fairly large red square appear where the ImageView control has been placed.

Notice the ImageView control has been automatically resized to show the Bitmap.

The ImageView control has a range of methods similar to setImageBitmap that makes it useful for displaying a range of different types of graphic.

Canvas

You can just use a Bitmap and work with individual pixels, but this isn't a very "high level" way to create graphics. What we need are some larger scale methods that draw useful things like lines, rectangles, circles and so on.

The Bitmap object doesn't have this sort of method but the Canvas object does and you can use it to draw on any Bitmap. That is you create a Canvas object, associate it with a Bitmap, and you can use the Canvas object's methods to draw on the Bitmap. There are lots of different Canvas drawing methods, and even a facility to transform the basic coordinate system to anything you care to use, but we have to start somewhere so a simple example first.

You can create a Canvas and attach it to a bitmap in one operation:

```
Canvas c = new Canvas(b);
```

Now when you use the drawing methods of the Canvas they draw on the Bitmap b. There are many occasions when a control or object provides a Canvas object attached to a Bitmap all ready for you to draw on.

It is also important to know that, initially, the coordinate system of the Canvas object is set to pixels as determined by the Bitmap. That is, if the Bitmap is *width* by *height* pixels, the default coordinate system runs from 0,0 at the top left-hand corner to *width*,*height* at the bottom right.

Using Canvas can be as simple as calling a method like drawLine to draw a line between two points. The only slight complication is that you have to use the Paint object to specify how the line will be drawn. In general Paint controls how any line or area is drawn by the Canvas methods.

A typical Paint object is something like:

```
Paint paint = new Paint();
paint.setAntiAlias(true);
paint.setStrokeWidth(6F);
paint.setColor(Color.BLUE);
paint.setStyle(Paint.Style.STROKE);
```

After creating the Paint object we set AntiAlias to true, i.e turn it on. This creates a higher quality but slightly slower rendering, and set the width of the line to 6 pixels, color to blue and set it as a stroke, i.e. a line rather than an area fill. If you are puzzled by the 6F in the setStrokeWidth it is worth saying that this is how you specify a float constant in Java.

Once created you can use a Paint object as often as it is needed and you can modify it and reuse it. You can also use an existing Paint object to create a new Paint object which you then modify.

A First Graphic

Now we have a Paint object we can draw a line:

```
c.drawLine(0F, 0F, 500F, 500F, paint);
```

This draws a line from 0,0 to 500,500 and as the Bitmap is 500 by 500 pixels this draws a diagonal line across the entire bitmap. Again the numeric values all end in F because the method needs float values, for reasons that will become clear later.

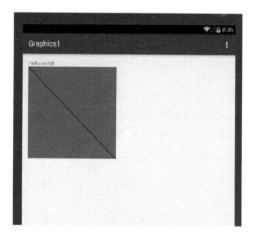

All you have to do now is get to know the different drawing methods provided. Here we use a few of the most common.

First we need to set the Paint object we created earlier to a FILL style so that we draw solid blocks of color and not just outlines:

```
paint.setStyle(Paint.Style.FILL);
```

To draw a yellow circle all we need is:

```
paint.setColor(Color.YELLOW);
c.drawCircle(400F, 200F, 50F, paint);
```

The first two parameters give the position of the center and the third is the circle's radius.

To draw a green rectangle:

```
paint.setColor(Color.GREEN);
c.drawRect(20F, 300F, 180F, 400F, paint);
```

The first two parameters give the top left hand corner and the next two the bottom right hand corner.

Finally let's add some text:

```
paint.setColor(Color.BLACK);
paint.setTextSize(50F);
c.drawText("Hello Graphics",0,14,90,80,paint);
```

The Paint object has a number of properties that let you set the font and style. In this example we simply set the text size. The drawText method takes a string, the start and end positions of characters in the string that will be displayed, and the coordinates of the starting location.

If you put this all together and run it you get this very tasteful graphic:

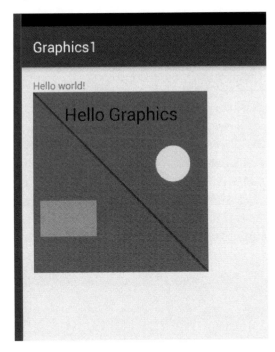

The complete code to create this is:

```
@Override
protected void onCreate(Bundle savedInstanceState) {

    super.onCreate(savedInstanceState);
    setContentView(R.layout.activity_main);

    Bitmap b = Bitmap.createBitmap(500, 500,Bitmap.Config.ARGB_8888);
    b.eraseColor(Color.RED);
    Canvas c = new Canvas(b);
    c = new Canvas(b);

    Paint paint = new Paint();
    paint.setAntiAlias(true);
    paint.setStrokeWidth(6f);
    paint.setColor(Color.BLUE);
    paint.setStyle(Paint.Style.STROKE);

    c.drawLine(0.0F, 0.0F, 500.0F, 500.0F, paint);

    paint.setStyle(Paint.Style.FILL);
    paint.setColor(Color.YELLOW);
    c.drawCircle(400F, 200F, 50F, paint);

    paint.setColor(Color.GREEN);
    c.drawRect(20F, 300F, 180F, 400F, paint);

    paint.setColor(Color.BLACK);
    paint.setTextSize(50F);
    c.drawText("Hello Graphics",0,14,90,80,paint);

    ImageView imageview=(ImageView) findViewById(R.id.imageView);
    imageview.setImageBitmap(b);
}
```

You can use this to try out other Canvas graphics methods.

If is worth pointing out that there is a set of drawBitmap methods that you can use to draw an existing Bitmap onto the Bitmap associated with the Canvas. This might seem like a strange thing to do but it is one of the most useful drawing operations because you can us it to implement simple sprite animation.

Transformations

Now we come to one of the more sophisticated options that Canvas offers. Before anything is drawn, the coordinates you supply are acted on by a transformation matrix. By default this is set to the identity matrix which leaves the coordinates as they were. However, the following methods modify the transformation matrix:

- rotate(float degrees)
  rotate about the origin through degrees

- rotate(float degrees, float px, float py)
  rotate about the point px,py through degrees

- scale(float sx, float sy)
  scale about the origin by sx and sy

- scale(float sx, float sy, float px, float py)
  scale about the point px,py by sx and sy

- skew(float sx, float sy)
  skew by sx and sy

- translate(float dx, float dy)
  translate by dx and dy.

There are also some methods that let you work directly with the transformation matrix:

- setMatrix(Matrix matrix)
  set the transform to the matrix provided

- concat(Matrix matrix)
  multiply the transform matrix by the matrix provided.

- getMatrix(Matrix m)
  get the transformation matrix in m

- getMatrix()
  return a copy of the transformation matrix

If you already know how matrices and transformation matrices work then this will be seem quite straightforward. If not, there are a lot of traps waiting to trip you up. The main one, that troubles just about everyone at first, is that the order in which you do things matters. A translation followed by a rotation isn't the same thing as a rotation followed by a translation. Try it if you don't believe me. Another is that these transformations change the coordinate system and don't affect anything you have already drawn. They only change what happens when you draw something after the transformation has been applied.

For example:

```
paint.setColor(Color.GREEN);
c.drawRect(20F, 300F, 180F, 400F, paint);

c.rotate(15F);
paint.setColor(Color.BLACK);
paint.setTextSize(50F);
c.drawText("Hello Graphics",0,14,90,80,paint);
```

In this case there is a 15 degree rotation after the rectangle has been drawn and before the text is drawn. The result is that the rectangle stays where it was but the text is rotated.

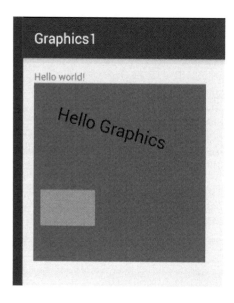

After the rotation everything you draw will be at 15 degrees.

Notice that the rotation is about the origin, i.e. 0,0 the top left hand corner. If you want to rotate about a different point, usually the center of some object, you need to use rotate(d,x,y).

For example to rotate the rectangle about its center you would use:

```
paint.setColor(Color.GREEN);
c.rotate(45,100,350);
c.drawRect(20F, 300F, 180F, 400F, paint);
```

where 100,350 is the center of the rectangle:

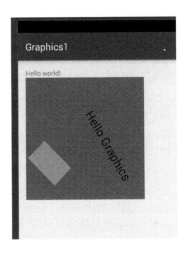

You can also see that the text is now in a different position and not simply rotated about the origin. This is because the 15 degree rotation is added to the 45 degree rotation around the center of the rectangle. To keep your transformations separate and non-interacting you have to remember to return the transformation matrix to the identity after you have changed it to something else.

How do you set the matrix back to the identity?

You could use:

```
c.setMatrix(new Matrix());
```

as Matrix() creates an identity matrix by default, or you could just use:

```
c.setMatrix(Null);
```

because passing a Null causes the matrix to be reset. However, needing to make a change to the transformation matrix and then restore the original is such a common operation that Canvas supports:

```
c.save()
```

which saves the current matrix and:

```
c.restore()
```

which restores the current matrix.

185

For example:

```
paint.setColor(Color.GREEN);

c.save();
c.rotate(45, 100, 350);
c.drawRect(20F, 300F, 180F, 400F, paint);

c.restore();
c.rotate(15F);

paint.setColor(Color.BLACK);
paint.setTextSize(50F);
c.drawText("Hello Graphics",0,14,90,80,paint);
```

With the save before the first rotate, the restore before the second decouples the two transformations.

A Logical Approach to Transforms

One approach to keeping track of transformations is to draw everything centered on the origin, and then translate, scale and rotate it to its final position. For example, to draw the rectangle:

```
c.drawRect(20F, 300F, 180F, 400F, paint);
```

you would first draw a unit square centered on the origin:

```
c.drawRect(-0.5F, -0.5F, 0.5F, 0.5F, paint);
```

then you would then scale it to its desired size:

```
c.scale(160,100);
```

and rotate it:

```
c.rotate(45F);
```

Finally you would move it to its correct location:

```
c.translate(100F, 350F);
```

If you try out these steps, you will discover that you don't get what you expect. The reason is that we have been transforming the object: draw a square, scale the square, rotate it and move it to the desired location. However, the Canvas transformations don't transform graphical objects but the coordinate system. You can immediately see that this means you should draw the square last after you have performed all of the transformations.

Indeed this is the rule:

- do everything you would have done to the geometric shape in the reverse order when changing the coordinate system.

So the correct transformation sequence is:

```
c.save();
c.translate(100F, 350F);
c.rotate(45F);
c.scale(160,100);
c.drawRect(-0.5F, -0.5F, 0.5F, 0.5F, paint);
c.restore();
```

You can always work out the transformation sequence you need by considering the graphical object, working out the transforms needed to change it to what you want and applying them in the reverse order.

Some programmers take to this idea and think it is the best and only way to do logical systematic graphics. Some adopt it a little bit and others draw things where they are needed in the size and orientation needed.

Setting Your Own Coordinates

When you first attach a Canvas to a Bitmap the coordinate system is in terms of the number of pixels in the Bitmap. Often, however, you want to work with a different coordinate system. For example, you might want to work with the origin in the middle and the x and y coordinate ranging from -1 to +1.

You can set any coordinate system you care to work with using suitable transformations.

If your coordinate system runs from xmin to xmax and from ymin to ymax you can apply it to the canvas using:

```
c.scale(width/(xmax-xmin),height/(ymax-ymin));
c.translate(-xmin,-ymin);
```

where *width* and *height* are the size in pixels of the bitmap.

Using this formulation the y coordinate increases down the screen, as did the original pixel coordinates.

If you want the y coordinate to increase up the screen then use the transformation:

```
c.scale(width/(xmax-xmin),-height/(ymax-ymin));
c.translate(-xmin,-ymax);
```

and notice the change to ymax in the second line.

So, for example, if you wanted to draw a graph using coordinates between 0,0 in the bottom left corner and 10,10 in the top right, i.e. y increasing up the screen, you would use:

```
c.save();
float xmax=10;
float xmin=0;
float ymax=10;
float ymin=0;
float width=500;
float height=500;

c.scale(width / (xmax - xmin), -height / (ymax - ymin));
c.translate(-xmin, -ymax);

paint.setStrokeWidth(.4f);
c.drawLine(0F, 0F, 10F, 0F, paint);
c.drawLine(0F, 0F, 0F, 10F, paint);
c.drawLine(0F, 0F, 10F, 10F, paint);
c.restore();
```

This draws axes and a 45 degree line:

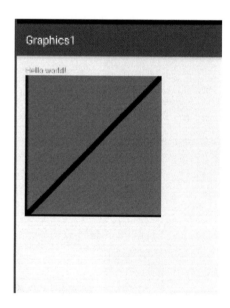

Notice that when you change the coordinate system all other measurements change as well. Hence the stroke width has to be set to 0.4 as it is no longer in terms of pixels.

Simple Animation

To bring this chapter to a close we will animate a ball bouncing around a Canvas, or a Bitmap depending how you look at it. This might seem like a strange topic to end on, especially since we are not going to do the job in the way that most Android programmers would go about it. Indeed Android has a range of different animation facilities - View animation, value animation and so on. However, none of them demonstrates the fundamental way that dynamic graphics work and before you move on to learn more sophisticated ways of creating animation it is a good idea to find out how things work at the lowest level.

This example not only teaches you something about animation, but also about the problems of creating dynamic graphics of any kind in the Android UI. One warning - do not assume this is all there is to know about Android animation or that this is the best way to do things.

To animate something in the simplest and most direct way all you have to do is draw the shape, change the shape, erase the old graphic, and draw it again.

In most systems this is usually achieved at the lowest possible level by using a timer to call an update function which erases the shape, does the update to the shape and then draws it at its new location. You can take this approach in Android, but for various reasons it isn't the way things are usually done. It has to be admitted that there are some slight difficulties, but overcoming them isn't hard and is very instructive.

To see how it all works let's just bounce a "ball" around the screen. This is more or less the "hello world" of simple 2D sprite-based graphics.

So start a new Android Studio project and place an ImageView on the design surface. This is the only UI element we need.

In the OnCreate method, after the UI has been expanded, all we need to do is set things up a bit more:

```
Bitmap b= Bitmap.createBitmap(width,height,Bitmap.Config.ARGB_8888);
c = new Canvas(b);
c.drawColor(Color.WHITE);
```

First we create a bitmap, associate it with a Canvas and then set the whole bitmap to white. Notice that other parts of the program are going to need to access width, height and c so they are defined as global variables:

```
private int width=800, height=800;
private Canvas c;
```

We are also going to need global variables to record the ball's position, its radius and velocity. For simplicity we might as well just use the default pixel coordinates of the Bitmap:

```
private float x=463,y=743,vx=1,vy=1,r=30;
```

Other functions are also going to need to access the ImageView control so it might as well be a global variable so that we don't have to waste time finding it each time it is needed:

```
private ImageView imageview;
```

and for the same reason a global Paint object saves time:

```
private Paint paint;
```

Now we have all of these variables defined we can move on with the OnCreate function and set up the Paint object:

```
paint = new Paint();
paint.setAntiAlias(false);
paint.setStyle(Paint.Style.FILL);
```

You might be wondering why AntiAlias is set to false, i.e. turned off. The reason is that its dithering algorithm makes it hard to remove a graphic by redrawing it in the background color. Try changing false to true in the final program to see what the problem is.

We also need to get the ImageView object and set the bitmap we are drawing on to display:

```
imageview=(ImageView) findViewById(R.id.imageView);
imageview.setImageBitmap(b);
```


Timer and Threads

Now we come to the inner workings of the animation. We need a Timer object that runs a function every so many milliseconds:

```
Timer timer=new Timer();
```

The timer object has a range of schedule functions which run a function, actually a TimerTask, at different times. The one we need is:

```
timer.schedule(TimerTask,delay,repeat);
```

which runs the TimerTask after *delay* milliseconds and every *repeat* milliseconds after that. The timings aren't accurate and it could take longer than specified for the TimerTask to be run.

The simplest way to create the TimerTask is to use an anonymous class:

```
timer.schedule(
 new TimerTask(){
  @Override
  public void run() {
   update();
  }
 }
 ,0,10 );
```

190

This creates a new TimerTask and overrides its run method. The run method is called when the Timer is triggered. All it does is to call a new function update, which we have yet to write, that does the update to the ball's position etc. The final two parameters specify a 0 millisecond delay in triggering the first call and then 10 milliseconds as the repeat period. That is, update will be called every 10 milliseconds or so. If the processor is busy doing something else it could be more than 10 milliseconds between repeats.

The update function is fairly easy:

```
void update(){
 paint.setColor(Color.WHITE);
 c.drawCircle(x, y, r, paint);

 x=x+vx;
 y=y+vy;

 if(x+r>=width)vx=-vx;
 if(x-r<=0)vx=-vx;
 if(y+r>=height)vy=-vy;
 if(y-r<=0)vy=-vy;

 paint.setColor(Color.RED);
 c.drawCircle(x, y, r, paint);
 imageview.invalidate();
}
```

First it sets the color to white and draws the ball, a circle. This erases the ball at its old position, remember the background is white. Next it updates the position by adding the velocities in each direction. To make sure that the ball bounces we test to see if it has reached a boundary and if it has its velocity is reversed. Finally, the color is set to red and the ball is drawn at the new position.

If the function was to stop at this point then everything compiles and runs, but you won't see the ball move. The reason is simply that the UI is drawn once at when the program is initially run and then only when it is necessary because the user has interacted with it or the orientation has changed, etc. As a result the bitmap displayed by the ImageView object would be changed every 10 milliseconds, but it would not be redisplayed.

To make the UI update we need to call the ImageView's invalidate method which basically tells the UI to redraw it. However if you put this in at the end of the update function you get an error message something like:

> *android.view.ViewRootImpl$CalledFromWrongThreadException: Only the original thread that created a view hierarchy can touch its views.*

The reason for this is that the Timer object uses a new thread to run the TimerTask. This is often what you want to happen, but in this case it is a problem. It is a problem that often occurs in creating a sophisticated Android app and something you are going to have to learn to cope with.

If you are new to the idea of threading, this explanation might help.

When you run an Activity it is assigned a single thread or execution. A thread is a unit of execution and it is what obeys your instructions. In a complete system there are many threads of execution - some running and some suspended. The operating system picks which threads get to run in a way that attempts to make them all seem to be making progress.

The single thread that the Activity gets is generally called the UI thread because its job is just to take care of the UI. It responds to events from the Activity like OnCreate and from the user like a Button click. When the UI thread responds to an event it obeys the event handler and then goes back to waiting for the next event. This is the sense in which every Android app is simply a collection of event handlers that the UI thread executes when the corresponding event occurs.

The big problem is that the UI event is really only happy when it has nothing to do. Then it just waits for an event and processes it at once. This makes the user think your app is very responsive because clicks and other input are acted on at once. If you give the UI thread a long task to do, for example you write a lot of processing into an event handler, then it isn't just waiting for the user to do something and the user starts to think that your app is slow and sluggish. At the extreme the UI thread can be kept 100% busy doing something and then the entire UI seems to freeze up.

*In short the UI thread should not be used for intensive computation or anything that takes more than a few milliseconds. The way to achieve this is to use other threads. This is a main topic of **Android Programming: Structuring Complex Apps.***

The UI thread creates the UI and to avoid problems of synchronization only the UI thread can interact with the UI. That is only the UI thread can access the UI. This is a fairly common approach to implementing a UI and not at all unique to Android.

So what happens is that the Timer tries to run its TimerTask and this in turn runs the update function, but using the thread the Timer runs on rather than the UI thread. Everything is fine until the last instruction of update, which attempts to use a method that belongs to an ImageView object and this it cannot do because it is not the UI thread. Hence the error message.

At this point many Android programmers give up and try a completely different approach. Some of these approaches do have advantages, see the Handler class for example for a good alternative. However the Android framework provides a method for just such a situation:

```
runOnUiThread(Runnable);
```

This is a method of the Activity object and you can use it from any thread that has access to the Activity object's methods to run a function on the UI thread. If the thread happens to be the UI thread then no harm done, the function is just called. If it isn't the UI thread then the call will be deferred until the UI thread is available and then the function will be run. As always the function shouldn't keep the UI thread busy for too long or the UI will become sluggish or even freeze completely.

The Java Runnable object has a single run method that is the function that is executed on the UI thread. So what we need to do in the Timer routine is:

```
runOnUiThread(
 new Runnable() {
  @Override
  public void run() {
   update();
  }
 }
);
```

This ensures that update is run on the UI thread.

Putting this all together gives:

```
timer.schedule(
 new TimerTask(){
  @Override
  public void run() {
   runOnUiThread(
    new Runnable() {
     @Override
     public void run() {
      update();
     }
    }
   );
  }
},0,10 );
```

This looks like a mess of nesting and curly braces, but you should be able to follow the logic. If you want to make things look simpler, then define the Runnable, and perhaps even the TimerTask, as a new class.

Now when you run the program you will see the red ball bounce slowly and smoothly around the screen. How good the animation is depends what you run it on. On the emulator is can be slow and irregular; on a real device it should be fine.

Animation complete with a trail to show how the ball moves

Now you know at least one way to allow a non-UI thread interact with the UI. There are so many ways to implement animation that this is just one of many starting points, but with an understanding of this one the others will seem easier. Even if you wanted to use this approach, the structure of this demonstration program could be improved. For example, the ball really should be a Ball class complete with its position and velocity properties and its update method. This way you gain the benefits of object-orientation and you can animate lots of balls around the screen with very little extra effort.

Listing

The complete listing of the animation program is:

```
import android.graphics.Bitmap;
import android.graphics.Canvas;
import android.graphics.Color;
import android.graphics.Paint;
import android.support.v7.app.ActionBarActivity;
import android.os.Bundle;
import android.view.Menu;
import android.view.MenuItem;
import android.widget.ImageView;
import java.util.Timer;
import java.util.TimerTask;
```

```java
public class MainActivity extends ActionBarActivity {
 private int width=800, height=800;
 private float x=463,y=743,vx=1,vy=1,r=30;
 private Canvas c;
 private Paint paint;
 private ImageView imageview;

 @Override
 protected void onCreate(Bundle savedInstanceState) {
  super.onCreate(savedInstanceState);
  setContentView(R.layout.activity_main);
  Bitmap b=Bitmap.createBitmap(width,height,
                                    Bitmap.Config.ARGB_8888);
  c = new Canvas(b);
  c.drawColor(Color.WHITE);
  paint = new Paint();
  paint.setAntiAlias(true);
  paint.setStyle(Paint.Style.FILL);
  imageview=(ImageView) findViewById(R.id.imageView);
  imageview.setImageBitmap(b); Timer timer=new Timer();

  timer.schedule(
   new TimerTask(){
    @Override
    public void run() {
     runOnUiThread(
      new Runnable() {
       @Override
       public void run() {
        update();
       }
      }
     );
    }
   },0,10 );
 }

 void update(){
  paint.setColor(Color.WHITE);
  c.drawCircle(x, y, r, paint);
  x=x+vx;
  y=y+vy;
  if(x+r>=width)vx=-vx;
  if(x-r<=0)vx=-vx;
  if(y+r>=height)vy=-vy;
  if(y-r<=0)vy=-vy;
  paint.setColor(Color.RED);
  c.drawCircle(x, y, r, paint);
  imageview.invalidate();
 }
}
```

There is so much to learn about graphics it is difficult to pick out things you need to know. If you want to find out more about how the standard UI works you need to look into the OnDraw event and how to create your own View object that render graphics. You need to find out about Android's vector graphics using shapes and path. You need to know about the different types of animation that are available and eventually you need to learn about OpenGL and its support for hardware accelerated 2D and 3D graphics.

Summary

- The subject of Android graphics is huge and there is always more than one way to approach any task. This chapter is a first look at what you might call UI-based graphics.

- The Bitmap is the basic graphics object. It consists of a rectangle of pixels that can be set to any color.

- The ImageView is a general purpose UI component that can be used to display a range of graphics objects including a Bitmap.

- You can draw on a Bitmap using a Canvas object which has a large number of different drawing methods.

- The color and drawing style used by many of the Canvas methods is determined by the properties of a Paint object.

- The Canvas object also supports transformations which can be used to modify where a graphic is drawn, its size, rotation etc.

- Transformations can be used to standardize the drawing of graphics objects at the origin.

- Transformations can also be used to change the default pixel coordinate system to anything you want to use.

- Simple animation is possible using nothing but a Bitmap, Canvas and an ImageView

- Only the UI thread can modify the UI.

- The Android Timer can be used to animate 2D graphics, but you have ensure that it runs the code on the UI thread using the RunOnUIThread method.

Chapter 12

Life Cycle Of An Activity

One of the things that you have to get used to when programming for a mobile platform is that your app can be shut down and restarted without much warning. This is something that often causes beginners and programmers from other platforms to make mistakes. You have to learn how to cope with this start-stop existence and that, for an Android app, it is a tough life just trying to stay alive.

I recently encountered an Android app, created by a large well known company, that asked me to fill in a form. I was just about to press the Submit button when I accidentally tilted the phone and the screen auto-rotated. When I looked again there was a blank form! I had to start over and, being a programmer ,I couldn't resist testing to see if the data vanished from the form when I rotated the phone a second time - it did! The programmers from this high-profile company had no idea about creating an Android app beyond the basics.

Don't fall into the same trap. Find out about app lifetime, state and persisting data. It may sound like a boring topic but it is vital to the working of a UI.

Lifetime and State

Most programmers are used to the idea that their application will be started by the user, used and then terminated by the user. If the application is restarted then it is usually up to the user to load whatever context they need by way of documents, etc. Sometimes an application has to automatically retain state information from run to run. For example, a game might keep track of which level a player had reached and the cumulative score, but this is about as complicated as things get.

For an application running on a mobile device things are very different. The very nature of the device means that any application could be interrupted at any moment by an incoming phone call or the user making a phone call. To a certain extent this need to make app "interruptible" has been taken up by mobile phone operating systems as a more general principle. Android, for example, will stop your application running just because it needs the memory or wants to save battery life. It even terminates and restarts your application if a media reconfiguration is required.

For example, as we discovered in a previous chapter, if the user changes the orientation of the device then your app is terminated and restarted. This is not quite a restart from scratch because the system saves and restores some state information automatically but exactly how all this works is something we have to find out.

The bottom line is that when you program under Android - and most other mobile operating systems - you have to care about the life cycle of your app and you have to take steps to ensure that its state is preserved so it can seem to the user that nothing at all has happened - even though your app has effectively been hit on the head and disposed of before being dragged back to continue from where it was.

Being an Android app is a dangerous existence and not at all like a Windows or a Linux app which can behave as if they have the machine all to themselves.

The Life Cycle Of An App

The different states that an Android app can be in and the transitions between them can seem complicated - that's because they are. If you are still thinking in terms of a desktop app that starts, runs and is terminated by the user, this level of complexity can seem unnecessary - and perhaps it is. However these are the rules that we have to play by.

The Activity class has a set of overridable event handlers for each of six states an Activity can be in. These work in pairs, bracketing the start and stop of the Activity:

- **onCreate and onDestroy** bracket the entire life of the Activity in memory and can be considered to be at the outermost level.
  This pair is called when the app is loaded into memory or unloaded from memory and bracket the entire lifetime of an Activity. When it is first loaded the onCreate is triggered and when the app is disposed of onDestroy is triggered. You clearly have to use these two to setup and destroy and resources which are needed for the entire lifetime of the app. However if your app is removed by the system it will call onDestroy just before unloading the Activity and onCreate when it reloads it. This means that onCreate may be called when you need to restore the state of the Activity so that the user doesn't notice any interruption.

- **onStart and onStop** bracket any period that the app is visible.
  It could be that the Activity is behind, say, a modal dialog box. The Activity is visible but not interacting with the user. This pair of events can be triggered multiple times during the entire lifetime of the app. Simple apps can mostly ignore the onStart and onStop events because

the Activity is still in memory and doesn't lose any resources or state. The main use of onStart and onStop is to give the app an opportunity to monitor any changes that might affect it while not interacting with the user. To confuse the issue even more there is also an **onRestart** event which occurs before the onStart event but only if this isn't the first time the Activity has fired the onStart - that is this is a true restart.

- **onResume and onPause** bracket the period that the Activity is in the foreground and interacting with the user.
  Again this pair of events can happen multiple times during the entire lifetime. The onResume event occurs when the Activity returns to the foreground and doing its usual job. The onPause event occurs when the user switches away to another app for example.

The Simple Approach

At this point you have every right to be confused with so many changes of status and having to respond to each one. The main thing to worry about is the complete restart of your app which triggers an onDestroy and an onCreate. This is the only one that destroys the current state of the app, the others are simply opportunities for your app to reduce the load on the system or to save some user data just in case. As the onDestroy is usually just an opportunity to clean up resources to avoid leaks, most simple apps really only have to handle the onCreate event.

It is tempting to think that this starting and stopping is just like a desktop app being terminated and then the user deciding to use it again, so that it's fine for the app to start off as if it was being run for the first time. In the case of an Android app this isn't what the user expects at all. Your app can be terminated by the system without the user knowing anything about it. When the user tries to regain access to an app they will generally expect it to carry on from where they left it. It may be a complete restart as far as you are concerned, but the user just switched to another app for a few minutes and expects to find yours as they left it.

What this means is that you cannot think about onCreate as if it was the constructor for your app. When onCreate is fired it might be the first time your program has ever run or it might be a restart with some things that you created on a previous start still in existence. For simple applications you can often simply create everything again as if it was the first time your app had run and in some cases you need to test the savedInstanceState to see if you are actually just restarting.

Notice also that often these events also tend to occur in sequences. For example, an app that has just received the onPause event is likely to go on to receive the onDestroy event because the system will remove it to free up memory. It is a mistake to try to think too much about sequences of events and ask which one should do any particular initialization or clean up. Just think about the state that your app is moving into and place the necessary code into that event handler.

Lifecycle Explorer

There is no better way to feel comfortable with the life cycle and its events than to write a short demo program that shows you when they occur.

Start a new Android Basic Activity project, accepting all defaults, and call it Lifecycle and then accept all the defaults to get started quickly. In the Designer remove the "Hello World" string and place a TextView on the design surface. Next resize it so that it fills most of the area and remove its default text entry.

The code we need is fairly easy, the only trick is to remember to call each of the system-provided event handler's that you have overridden. If you don't do this the app simply terminates when you run it.

The OnCreate event handler still has to construct the UI, but now we get a reference to the Java object representing the TextView into a global variable so that the event handlers can access it:

```
private TextView textView;
@Override
protected void onCreate(Bundle savedInstanceState) {
  super.onCreate(savedInstanceState);
  setContentView(R.layout.activity_main);
  textView = (TextView) findViewById(R.id.textView);
  textView.append("Create\n");
}
```

The rest of the program simply overrides each of the event handlers in turn, calls the original event handler and then adds a text message to textView:

```
@Override
protected void onStart() {
 super.onStart();
 textView.append("Start\n");
}
@Override
protected void onPause() {
 super.onPause();
 textView.append("Pause\n");
}
@Override
protected void onResume() {
 super.onResume();
 textView.append("Resume\n");
}
@Override
protected void onStop() {
 super.onStop();
 textView.append("Stop\n");
}
@Override
protected void onRestart() {
 super.onRestart();
 textView.append("Restart\n");
}
@Override
protected void onDestroy() {
 super.onDestroy();
 textView.append("Destroy\n");
}
```

A very simple and tedious sort of program.

Trying It Out

If you now run this program you can use it to find out when the life cycle events happen. You might be surprised to learn that when you first run the program you get:

If you think about it for a moment this isn't unreasonable as the app is being loaded, becoming visible and in the foreground, and hence the appropriate events are fired in turn.

Beginners often assume that the life cycle events some how override each other. That is, if an onCreate has been fired then this is the big event in the Activity's life and so the others won't happen. This is isn't the case and you need to make sure that you put actions into the event handlers that really are appropriate to the life cycle state. For example, if you put something in the onResume event handler make sure you realize that it is going to be fired when the app first starts up as well as when it just being resumed.

If you try other things, like pressing the Home key and selecting another app, then you will see other event sequences, but of course only when you resume the Lifecycle app.

For example pressing the Home key, then showing the task manager by long pressing the Home key and reselecting your app results in: Pause, Stop as the app is removed from the foreground and then Restart, Start, Resume as the app is loaded, becomes visible and then resumes the foreground and interacts with the user.

You can try other actions out but there is one thing you must try out - changing the orientation. If you are using the emulator then press Ctrl-F11. When the screen orientation changes you will see that the TextView has been cleared and Create, Start, Resume have been added.

This is because when you change orientation the app is completely stopped and then completely restarted, i.e. it is as if the app was being run from scratch for the first time.

This statement is almost true - but not quite.

Retaining State - The Bundle

When you change orientation your app is stopped and restarted. When this happens the TextView is reset to its default state when the app loads. This description of what is happening is perhaps what you might expect. However this isn't the complete story.

The system does try to help you with the problem of having your app stopped in its tracks and restarted. It will automatically retain the state of UI elements that can be modified by the user and it automatically restores them when the app starts. So in principle you can initially ignore the problem of an app restart because the system restores your UI. This is the reason that some Android programmers assume that everything is "normal" and there is no need to study the lifecycle of an app. This is true at first but later your app will evolve beyond what the system provides by default.

Automatically saving and restoring the UI's state is what the **savedInstanceState** parameter in the onCreate event handler is all about:

```
protected void onCreate(Bundle savedInstanceState) {
```

A Bundle is a set of key value pairs which is used to save the values stored in UI elements when the app is stopped by the system. It stores id/value pairs and when the app is restarted the Bundle is used to initialize the values in the corresponding UI elements. Notice that if the user stops your app by removing it from the recent apps list then the savedInstanceState is destroyed and the app really does start over afresh and the onCreate isn't passed a Bundle to restore the UI. In other words, savedInstanceState only restores the UI when the app has been stopped by the system.

It is also worth noticing that the restore will work to an alternative layout loaded because of a configuration change. For example, it will restore state to a landscape version of a layout as well as the original portrait version. All that matters is that the current layout has View objects with the correct ids.

At this point you are probably wondering why the TextView object wasn't restored by the system when then device was rotated? The simple answer is that a TextView object isn't intended for user interaction - it is supposed to just be used to show static text labels and so the system doesn't save and restore it.

You can see the automatic save and restore in action if you add an EditText input field on the design surface of the Lifecycle Explorer. Now if you enter some text into the EditText field it will be retained if you rotate the device. However if you press and hold the Home key, remove the app and then start it afresh you will see that the EditText field is blank again.

The text in the EditText field at the bottom of the screen is preserved during a screen rotation.

- The general principle is that any UI element that can be modified by the user is automatically saved and restored. Any changes that your code makes or that the user makes in complex UI components are lost unless you take steps to preserve them.

Saving Additional UI Data

The system will save and restore the state of the UI elements that the user can change, but it will not store any that your code changes. It also doesn't automatically save and restore any other data that the user or your code may have generated that isn't within the UI. In these cases you have to write some code that saves the values and restores them.

There are lots of ways of saving the state of an app as it is started and stopped by the system. One of the simplest is to use the Bundle object that the system uses.

The system fires the **onSaveInstanceState** event when it is about to add data to the Bundle and save it. If you want to save some additional data all you have to do is override the default event handler. For example, suppose you want to save and restore the data in the TextView in the Lifecycle Explorer. First you have to save the data:

```
@Override
protected void onSaveInstanceState(Bundle savedInstanceState){
 savedInstanceState.putCharSequence("myText",textView.getText());
 super.onSaveInstanceState(savedInstanceState);
}
```

Notice that we save the text content of the textView object as the value and use the key "myText". In most cases it would be better to create a string constant for the key. The key can be any identifier you care to use but it has to be unique within the Bundle as it is used to retrieve the data you have stored in the Bundle.

Now to retrieve the data and place it into the TextView we need to change the onCreate event handler:

```
@Override
protected void onCreate(Bundle savedInstanceState) {
 super.onCreate(savedInstanceState);
 setContentView(R.layout.activity_main);
 textView = (TextView) findViewById(R.id.textView);
 if (savedInstanceState != null)    {
  textView.setText(savedInstanceState.getCharSequence("myText"));
 }
 textView.append("Create\n");
}
```

This starts off in the usual way but now we check to see if savedInstanceState has any data. If it does we retrieve the stored text using the key "myText".

There is no reason not to use the onCreate event handler in this way but the system also fires an **onResetoreInstanceState** event when it is about to perform its own "automatic" restore of the UI for you. You can override this event handler if you want to keep the code that restores the app's state kept out of the onCreate event handler.

For example, you could have written:

```
@Override
protected void onRestoreInstanceState(Bundle savedInstanceState) {
super.onRestoreInstanceState(savedInstanceState);
if (savedInstanceState != null) {
 textView.setText(savedInstanceState.getCharSequence("myText"));
 }
}
```

Do remember to call the **super.onRestoreInstanceState** if you want the system to restore the rest of the UI in the usual way. There are put and get methods for a range of standard data types. All simple types, byte, integer and so on, are supported, as are strings, arrays and other simple data structures. You can also create your own classes that can be stored in a Bundle by implementing the Parcelable interface. Notice you can save arbitrary data, and not just data for the layout. You can also create your own Bundle instance and make use of it for data storage, persistence and for transferring data to other parts of a program. There are many standard classes the Bundle doesn't support. In these cases you have to make your own arrangements to save data to storage.

Often all you need to do to make sure that your app maintains its state between system restarts is to use the savedInstanceState Bundle object. This approach also reduces much of the practicality of life cycle management to implementing the onSaveInstanceState and onRestoreInstanceState event handlers. This is so much simpler than having to worry about all of the different life cycle events.

As an exercise you can now go back to the iCalc example in Chapter 3 and make its display and current value persist through a screen rotate.

Complex UI Elements

One of the traps waiting for you is the problem of exactly what is automatically saved and restored. For example, at the start of this chapter we had the story of the app that lost the user's form data when it was rotated. Given what we now know of the auto-saving and restoration of user modifiable UI elements, you might be wondering how this could happen? The answer is that the programmers of the app had probably grown accustomed to the automatic persistence of UI state and didn't bother to check that rotation had no effect. It did have an effect because the form was being downloaded from a website and displayed in a WebView control. A WebView control is persisted by the system, but it reloads the page when it is restored. This means that on a rotation the form was reloaded as empty and the user's data was lost.

- You always have to check that things work as you expect. Always test what happens to your UI on a rotation.

Advanced State Management

For completeness it is worth noting that there are many more approaches to maintaining state. Later you will need to discover how to store lots of user data locally for longer term persistence and this is often enough to implement state management though a configuration change.

There are also more advanced state management problems when you come to make use of Fragments, the subject of *Android Programming: Mastering Fragments & Dialogs*. In this case you can use setRetainedInstance to ask the system not to destroy an entire Fragment. This means that all of the data stored in the Fragment is retained even though the Activity may be removed from memory. This makes it possible to use a Fragment as a repository of state.

The ultimate in making sure that things happen as you want it to handle the configuration change yourself. You can do this by making a change to the manifest. If you do this then it is up to you to make the changes needed when the **onConfigurationChanged** even occurs. You could, for example, opt to animate buttons and other UI objects into new positions or just ignore the need to reconfigure altogether.

This is all advanced and for most applications you can get by using just the onSaveInstanceState and onRestoreInstanceState event handlers.

Summary

- Android, like many other mobile OSs, will remove your app from memory and restart it as it needs to.

- The user will not be aware that your app has been destroyed and recreated and will expect it to continue from where they left off.

- The system signals changes in state to your Activity via a complicated set of events. You need to understand how these work in order to make your Activity resume correctly after the various levels of suspension.

- onCreate should not be regarded as the "constructor" for your app because it is called when the app is restored as well as when it is run for the first time.

- The system will store the state of any user modifiable UI components and restore it when the Activity resumes.

- The data is stored in a special instance of Bundle called savedInstanceState.

- The system alerts you when it is about to save and restore data from savedInstanceState by firing the onSaveInstanceState and onRestoreInstanceState event handlers.

- You can override both of these event handlers to save and restore extra data in the savedInstanceState Bundle.

- For many simple apps you can mostly ignore the life cycle events and concentrate on using the onSaveInstanceState and onRestoreInstanceState event handlers to persist data.

- You must always check that UI and other elements are persisted through a suspension of your app. You can test using a rotation configuration change.

- There are other more advanced ways of saving state which you will need to discover later on. You can't use a Bundle for everything.

Chapter 13

Spinners

Working with Android Studio makes building the UI easy with an interactive editor, the Designer, but you still need to find out how to handle the things it isn't quite so good at. In the next two chapters of our exploration of Android we look at spinners and pickers, the next step up from buttons and text controls.

Spinners are what are referred to as drop-down lists or something similar in other UIs. They allow the user to pick from a list of possible items. Pickers, which are the subject of Chapter 14, also allow the user to pick an item, but in this case the items are more narrowly defined - a date, a time or a number.

The Spinner And The Designer

- The spinner presents a set of alternatives to the user and lets them select one.

Putting a Spinner into you project is as easy as using the tool Palette in the Designer but you can't get away without some Java to make it all work. In particular, you need to define the list of items that the Spinner will display when the user activates it.

When you place a Spinner on the design surface all you get is a blank control with a non-functioning dropdown icon.

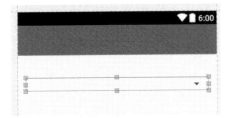

At the moment the Designer only provides minimal support for setting up the Spinner with some data to display. The simplest sort of thing to show the user is a list of text items and you might well think that the most direct way of doing this is to use a String array. It is but things are slightly more complicated than this. They are simple, however, if you create a resource to specify the String array because in this case the system will do everything necessary to load the data.

Setting the contents of the Spinner using a String array in code is a good way to see how the Spinner works but it isn't the way it usually happens.

Android provides a comprehensive system of resources - strings, images and lots of XML files. The idea is that you can produce customized versions of you application just by changing the resource files, i.e. without having to modify your code. For detailed information on using resources refer back to Chapter 10.

In the case of a Spinner you could set up a resource that was a String array that provided the list of items to be displayed. If you then wanted to create a version of your app for a foreign market you could get the list translated to create a resource in the new language.

Resources are a great idea and you should use them for all fixed strings and fixed data in general. So far, the examples have tended to avoid resources to make things simpler, but for a Spinner you need to know how to code up a String array resource and use it.

Android Studio does have some good resource support but in some areas it is lacking. For example, in an ideal world the system would help you create a String or String array resource, but at the moment it only only provides help for simple string values. It will help you create a String resource but offers no assistance for a String array, for which we have no choice but work with the XML file.

Find the file strings.xml in the res/values directory and open the file strings.xml. Add to this the String array definition:

```
<string-array name="country">
 <item>Canada</item>
 <item>Mexico</item>
 <item>USA</item>
</string-array>
```

The meaning of the XML is obvious and this is the advantage of a human readable markup language.

If you have explored resources using the Resource window which appears when you select the three dots option in the Properties window you might worry that this new resource, i.e. SpinnerList, doesn't appear. It also doesn't appear in the Resource editor that you can select while editing the XML file.

The reason is that, currently, Android Studio doesn't support the assignment, editing or creation of String Arrays other than manually. However making use of the new resource is fairly easy. The id of the resource is @array/country and this has to be typed into the entries property in the Properties window as the Resource picker doesn't support arrays at the moment.

If you enter the id correctly you will see the first item appear in the Spinner within the editor. When you run the app you will see all of the entries when you drop down the list:

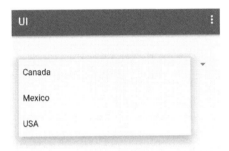

For simple lists of options that can be specified at design time this is all you need to know about how to load a list of items into a Spinner. In practice however a Spinner usually has to be loaded with a list at runtime and then you need to know about the ArrayAdapter.

Introducing the ArrayAdapter

In the case of UI widgets that display lists of things Android has a much more general mechanism to cope with the different type of things you could display. Widgets that show lists of things generally work with an example of an "adapter". For more on adapters in general see The Adapter in Chapter 15.

An adapter basically takes a list of objects and converts them into something that can be displayed in the widget. In general, you can create custom Adapters to do clever things with lists of objects of your own so that they display appropriately. In most cases, however, you can get by with just using the provided built-in adapters.

In the case of the spinner the most usual choice is the ArrayAdapter. This takes an array of objects of any type and makes them suitable for display by calling their **toString()** method. As long as the toString() method produces what you want to see in the Spinner then everything should work.

In the case of an array of Strings calling the toString() method on each array element might seem like overkill, but it is the price we pay to build mechanisms that can cope with more complicated situations.

So the plan of action is to create a String array with the items we want to display, use this to initialize an ArrayAdapter object and then attach the ArrayAdapter to the Spinner.

Creating the array is easy:

```
String[] country = {"Canada", "Mexico", "USA"};
```

The ArrayAdapter constructor can seem to be complicated. It seems even more complicated because ArrayAdapter uses generics to allow you to specify the type of each element in the array.

If you haven't used generics before, all you need to know is that, in general, generics are a way of creating useful classes, often collections of objects that can be of a type you specify. You know you are working with a generic when you have to specify the type it is to work with using <type>.

So instead of creating a special array Adapter for each type of array, an IntArrayAdapter, a StringArrayAdapter and so on, you simply have to specify the type as <int> or <String> when you use the generic ArrayAdapter type.

For example, to create an ArrayAdapter for an array of Strings you would use:

```
ArrayAdapter<String> stringArrayAdapter =
          new ArrayAdapter<String>(constructor parameters);
```

The pattern is the same for all the constructors and for different array types.

There are quite a few ArrayAdapter constructors, but they all need some basic information. They need to know the current context, usually this, and the layout to be used to display the list and the array of data items.

The only difficult one is the layout to be used to display the list. This sounds like a lot of hard work until you discover that the system provides some basic standard layouts that you can just use.

In our case the layout is:

```
android.R.layout.simple_spinner_dropdown_item
```

Notice that this is actually an integer that determines the layout resource to use and nothing more complicated. Putting it all together gives:

```
ArrayAdapter<String> stringArrayAdapter = new ArrayAdapter<String>(
          this,
          android.R.layout.simple_spinner_dropdown_item,
          country);
```

If you are wondering what country is, remember that we defined a String array called country earlier.

The final step is to specify the ArrayAdapter to use in the Spinner. First we have to retrieve the Spinner and then we can use its **setAdapter** method:

```
Spinner spinner=(Spinner)findViewById(R.id.spinner);
spinner.setAdapter(stringArrayAdapter);
```

If you add all of the code to the onCreate event handler the result is:

```
@Override
protected void onCreate(Bundle savedInstanceState) {
 super.onCreate(savedInstanceState);
 setContentView(R.layout.activity_main);
 String[] country={"Canada", "Mexico", "USA"};
 ArrayAdapter<String> stringArrayAdapter=new ArrayAdapter<String>(
      this,
      android.R.layout.simple_spinner_dropdown_item,
      country);
 Spinner spinner = (Spinner)  findViewById(R.id.spinner);
 spinner.setAdapter(stringArrayAdapter);
}
```

If you run the program you will see the same drop-down list we produced using just the Designer.

Handling the Selection

The next question is how do you discover that the user has made a selection?

The simple answer is that we have to hookup to the Spinner's events. As always there are three possible ways of doing this. Here's a quick recap:

- Create a sub-class of AdapterView.OnItemSelectedListener and then an instance
- Implement the AdapterView.OnItemSelectedListener interface as part of the Activity
- Use an anonymous class

Of the three the anonymous class nearly always seems the easiest because Android Studio will generate the interface methods for you.

If you start typing the following line and use Alt+Enter, to autocomplete:

```
AdapterView.OnItemSelectedListener onSpinner=
            new AdapterView.OnItemSelectedListener(){
```

Android Studio will generate:

```
AdapterView.OnItemSelectedListener onSpinner =
                new AdapterView.OnItemSelectedListener() {
 @Override
 public void onItemSelected(
  AdapterView<?> parent,
  View view,
  int position,
  long id) {
 }

 @Override
 public void onNothingSelected(
  AdapterView<?>  parent) {
 }
}
```

It also adds an import for AdapterView but you still need to add the required final semicolon. If you don't use autocomplete you have to type everything in, including the import.

You can see at once that you have to implement two event handlers:

- onItemSelected - triggered when the user selects an item
- onNothingSelected - triggered when the Spinner has no items or the user deselects all items

You might be surprised to see two occurrences of <?> in the generated code. Both events are generic and, as already explained, they can work with a range of different types. The <?> is a type wildcard which essentially allows any type to be used. For example List<?> is a list of any type. Of course, the actual type isn't known until runtime and so every element of the List is treated as an Object type and it's up to you to cast it to something more specific.

Let's look at the **onItemSelected** event handler in more detail:

```
public void onItemSelected(
  AdapterView<?> parent,
  View view,
  int position,
  long id) {
}
```

What is this AdapterView that has suddenly appeared? As explained in earlier chapters all of the visible components of the UI correspond to View objects of one sort or another. An AdapterView is the View object that corresponds to one of the displayed items in the Spinner. You could, for example, use the AdapterView passed to the event handler to modify the appearance of the displayed item.

The view parameter is just the child of the AdapterView that was actually clicked. Note that an item can be composed of more than one View item.

Finally the int position parameter and the long id provide the position of the view that was clicked in the adapter and the row id of the item that was selected.

You can populate a Spinner from a database. In this case the row id gives the database row number, which isn't necessarily the same as its position in the Spinner. For a simple ArrayAdapter the position and id are the same. In most cases the only parameter you will be interested in is the int position which gives you the item the user selected. For example, place a TextView on the design surface and change the onItemSelected event handler to read:

```
@Override
public void onItemSelected(
 AdapterView<?> parent,
 View view,
 int position,
 long id) {
  TextView myTextView = (TextView) findViewById(R.id.textView);
  myTextView.setText(Integer.toString(position));
}
```

All that happens is that the position parameter is displayed in the TextView.

Finally to connect the eventhandling object to the Spinner we need to add it using its **setOnItemSelectListener**:

```
spinner.setOnItemSelectedListener(onSpinner);
```

Putting all of this together gives the new onCreate:

```
@Override
protected void onCreate(
 Bundle savedInstanceState) {
 super.onCreate(savedInstanceState);

 AdapterView.OnItemSelectedListener onSpinner =
         new AdapterView.OnItemSelectedListener() {

 @Override
 public void onItemSelected(
  AdapterView<?> parent,
  View view,
  int position,
  long id) {
   TextView myTextView =  (TextView)findViewById(R.id.textView);
   myTextView.setText(Integer.toString(position));
 }
```

```
 @Override
 public void onNothingSelected(
   AdapterView<?> parent) {
 }
};

setContentView(R.layout.activity_main);
String[] country = {"Canada", "Mexico", "USA"};
ArrayAdapter<String> stringArrayAdapter=new ArrayAdapter<String>(
        this,
        android.R.layout.simple_spinner_dropdown_item,
        country);
 Spinner spinner = (Spinner) findViewById(R.id.spinner);
 spinner.setAdapter(stringArrayAdapter);
 spinner.setOnItemSelectedListener(onSpinner);
}
```

If you now run the program you will see something like:

The position displayed corresponds to the element in the array that has been selected, counting from zero of course.

Most of the time is it enough just to have the index number of the selected item, but the AdapterView object has a few methods that enable you to get the selected item. If you want to review the selected item you could use the position to index the original ArrayAdapter, or even the original String array, but these aren't generally available to the event handler. So to retrieve the item you would use the **getItemAtPosition** method. For example to display the country name you would modify the setText call to:

```
 myTextView.setText((String) parent.getItemAtPosition(position));
```

Notice that the selected item is returned as an object type and you have to cast it before you can do anything with it.

There are other methods that can be used to retrieve information or manipulate the selected element, but for most simple applications the getItemAtPosition is all you really need.

Creating An ArrayAdapter From A Resource

To create an ArrayAdapter from a resource you need to make use of a static method of the ArrayAdapter class, **createFromResource**. This just needs you to specify the context, the resource id and the Spinner layout. All you have to do is to replace the creation of stringArrayAdapter

```
ArrayAdapter<CharSequence> stringArrayAdapter=
    ArrayAdapter.createFromResource(
                this,
                R.array.country,
                android.R.layout.simple_spinner_dropdown_item);
```

With this change everything works as before, but now to change the items that appear in the Spinner you simply edit the XML file.

You could also use the **getResources** object to retrieve the String array and then proceed as if the String array had been defined in code.

```
private String[] country =
        getResources().getStringArray(R.array.SpinnerList);
```

Changing The List

There are lots of more advanced things that you can do with Spinners, but these aren't encountered that often and mainly occur when trying to build a custom user experience.

The one thing that does occur often is the need to dynamically change the list of items. There are many slight variations on this, but essentially what you do is change the String array and then call the adapter's **notifyDataSetChange** method. For example, if you want to change Mexico, i.e. element one, to Greenland you would use:

```
country[1]="Greenland";
stringArrayAdapter.notifyDataSetChanged();
```

The ArrayAdapter also has add, clear, remove and insert methods which can be used to modify the underlying data, but for this to work the object holding the data has to be modifiable.

You can't modify a String array in this way. What you need instead is an ArrayList. If you change the declaration of country to:

```
ArrayList<String> country=new ArrayList<String>(
                Arrays.asList("Canada", "Mexico", "USA"));
```

you can add "Greenland" to the end of the items using:

```
stringArrayAdapter.add("Greenland");
```

Notice that in this case the ArrayAdapter constructor used changes from one that accepts an array to one that accepts a List of objects.

You can always find out how many items there are using the **getCount** method.

How do you modify a list of items that are created using a resource? This is a tricky question because the ArrayAdapter creates a String array to hold the data which means you can't use the methods that modify a list. There are a number of ways of fixing this, but the simplest is to construct your own ArrayList from the resource directly:

```
Resources res=getResources();
ArrayList<String> country=new ArrayList<String>(
        Arrays.asList(res.getStringArray(R.array.SpinnerList)));
ArrayAdapter<String> stringArrayAdapter= new ArrayAdapter<String>(
        this,
        android.R.layout.simple_spinner_dropdown_item,
        country);
```

With this version of the ArrayAdapter you can once again use the add, and other methods, to modify the list of items.

Summary

- Spinners are a way of presenting a list of options for the user to select from.

- Spinners can be complex in terms of their layout and what they show, but the simplest example is to work with an array of Strings.

- The array of Strings can be created in the code or within a resource file.

- The array of Strings has to be converted into an ArrayAdapter object to be used with the Spinner.

- The ArrayAdapter provides a View object for each item displayed in the Spinner.

- There are two ways (at least) to load a String array resource into an ArrayAdapter - using its createFromResource or by loading the resource as String array and then proceeding as before.

- Loading the String array has the advantage that you can change it into an ArrayList, which can be modified in code by adding or deleting elements. You cannot change the length of a String array.

- To find out what the user has selected simply use the onItemSelected event handler.

- To retrieve the item that the user has selected use the getItemAtPosition(position) method.

Android currently supports three Pickers for dates, times and general numbers and they are important ways to get user input. However they have been through so many revisions that they lack simple documentation or guidelines how to use them. Let's clear up the confusion.

Working with Pickers

- A picker is a "dial" that you can use to select one of a predetermined set of values.

In this sense it is a lot like the Spinner covered in the previous chapter, but one that has a restricted set of choices.

There are two ways to make use of a Picker, as a widget, or as a dialog box. You will find the TimePicker and the DatePicker, ready to place on the design surface, in the Date&Time section of the Palette. The NumberPicker, however, is much lower down, in the Advanced section.

Although in some cases you probably will want to create a Dialog box and will need to use a complex DialogFragment to wrap the Dialog and manage its life cycle, and there are many situations where using the raw widget will do the job well enough. For more on DialogFragment see: ***Android Programming: Mastering Fragments & Dialogs***

TimePicker

The TimePicker is a very easy way to get started. If you create a new Android project, called TimeAndDate and accept all of the defaults you can place a TimePicker, listed top of the Date & Time section of the Palette, on the design surface just like any other widget and size and locate it as required. In its default configuration it shows in the Designer using the style android:timePickerStyle and has an analog clock face and an input area that can be used to set the time by dragging the hands on the clock face:

Pickers are complex widgets that have multiple components, each of which can change its appearance depending on how they are styled and which version of Android you are targeting. While you can select from a range of themes, they don't all work with all SDK/APIs and they may to be removed at some time in the future. For example, before API 14 this theme was used:

API 14 adopted the Holo theme and the picker looked like this:

What follows is what you get if you simply accept the defaults. However, it is important to realize that exactly what the user sees depends on the version of Android they are using. For example your up-to-date app running on the latest Android might look like the clock TimePicker but it you run it on a pre-Lollipop API such as Jelly Bean (API 18) then you will see the Holo-themed version as above. If you want to support older version then it is important to remember to test using them. If you want to use something that looks like the Holo-themed version on all versions then all you have to do is find timePickerMode in the Properties window and use the drop-down list to select spinner or clock depending on the type you need.

For easy backward compatibility use compatibility library v7 appcompat, which is included in your projects automatically by Android Studio, and stick with the AppCompat themes.

TimePicker In Code

To interact with the TimePicker all you have to use is the get/set methods for Hour and Minute. You can also programatically change the 12 hour/24 hour mode. Notice that the time is always returned in 24-hour form no matter what the widget's mode is.

Although the set/getCurrentMinute and set/getCurrentHour methods are deprecated, the alternatives which do exactly the same thing set/getMinute and set/getHour don't work on earlier versions of Android. So for the moment it seems preferable to use the deprecated methods and ignore the warnings. For example to set the TimePicker you would use;

```
TimePicker tp= (TimePicker) findViewById(R.id.timePicker);
tp.setIs24HourView(true);
tp.setCurrentMinute(10);
tp.setCurrentHour(13);
```

The only task remaining is figuring out how to discover then the user has selected a time.

You could provide a button which the user has to click to confirm the new time. For example, place a Button and a TextView on the design surface and add the following Button click event handler:

```
public void doButtonClick(View e){
 TextView tv= (TextView) findViewById(R.id.textView);
 TimePicker tp= (TimePicker) findViewById(R.id.timePicker);
 tv.setText(tp.getCurrentHour().toString() + ":"+
                          tp.getCurrentMinute().toString());
}
```

Also remember to set the Button's Click property to doButtonClick.

This provides a way for the user set the time:

In most cases the difficult part in using a Picker isn't setting it up or getting the data from it, but in processing that data into a form in which your program can use it. In this case we simply convert the time into a slightly formatted string representation.

Updating the time

What about getting an update every time the user changes the TimePicker? This requires an event handler for an OnTimeChanged event which can be implemented with an OnTimeChangedListener interface in the Activity or as an anonymous class.

Using Android Studio the anonymous class approach is usually better. If you type in:

```
TimePicker.OnTimeChangedListener OnTimeChanged=
                new TimePicker.OnTimeChangedListener() {
```

using Alt+Enter for code completion, Android Studio will generate a stub including the onTimeChanged method to which you can add your code:

```
TimePicker.OnTimeChangedListener OnTimeChanged=
                new TimePicker.OnTimeChangedListener() {
 @Override
 public void onTimeChanged(
      TimePicker view,
      int hourOfDay,
      int minute) {
 }
}
```

You can guess that when the time is changed by the user the onTimeChanged method is called and the TimePicker that triggered the event is passed as view, and its hour and minute setting as hourOfDay and minute and all that is now needed is to set the event handler using the setOnTimeChangedListener method.

For example, to transfer the new time to the TextView used in the previous example you would use:

```
TimePicker.OnTimeChangedListener OnTimeChanged =
                    new TimePicker.OnTimeChangedListener() {
  @Override
  public void onTimeChanged(
              TimePicker view,
              int hourOfDay,
              int minute) {

  TextView tv = (TextView) findViewById(R.id.textView);
  tv.setText(Integer.toString(hourOfDay) +
                    ":" + Integer.toString(minute));
  }
};
```

You also need to add:

```
tp.setOnTimeChangedListener(OnTimeChanged);
```

to OnCreate to associate the OnTimeChanged object and its event handling method with the TimePicker. Now if you run the program you will see the TextView change every time the user alters the TimePicker by whatever method.

The full program, including the code for the button and the event handler is shown below:

```
import android.support.v7.app.AppCompatActivity;
import android.os.Bundle;
import android.view.Menu;
import android.view.MenuItem;
import android.view.View;
import android.widget.TextView;
import android.widget.TimePicker;

public class MainActivity extends AppCompatActivity {
@Override
protected void onCreate(Bundle savedInstanceState) {
 super.onCreate(savedInstanceState);
 setContentView(R.layout.activity_main);
 TimePicker tp = (TimePicker) findViewById(R.id.timePicker);
 tp.setIs24HourView(true);
 tp.setCurrentMinute(10);
 tp.setCurrentHour(13);
 tp.setOnTimeChangedListener(OnTimeChanged);
}
```

```
Onpublic  void doButtonClick(View e) {
  TextView tv = (TextView)findViewById(R.id.textView);
  TimePicker tp = (TimePicker) findViewById(R.id.timePicker);
  tv.setText(tp.getCurrentHour().toString()
                  + ":" + tp.getCurrentMinute().toString());
 }

  TimePicker.OnTimeChangedListener OnTimeChanged =
                  new TimePicker.OnTimeChangedListener() {
  @Override
   public void onTimeChanged(
      TimePicker view,
      int hourOfDay,
      int minute) {
    TextView tv = (TextView) findViewById(R.id.textView);
    tv.setText(Integer.toString(hourOfDay) +
              ":" + Integer.toString(minute));
  }
 };
}
```

DatePicker

There are two date widgets in the current Android system DatePicker and
Calendar view. The DatePicker has been in use since API 1 but Calendar view
was only introduced in API 11. The main difference between the two is the
way that they look. As they work in much the same way and the DatePicker is
more versatile this is the widget we will use. Also once you have experienced
the way TimePicker work there is very little to add to cover its date
counterpart.

To see the DatePicker in action simply start a new project called Date and
accept all of the defaults. Place a DatePicker on the design surface at the top
left-hand corner. The DatePicker underwent the same changes with the
introduction of Material Design as did the TimePicker. As long as you use the
latest API and the default layout it will show in a calendar format:

As is the case with the TimePicker, if you run your app on an older pre-Lollipop version of Android then you will see the Holo-themed spinner version:

You can opt to display the Holo spinner version in all Android versions by setting the datePickerMode to spinner. As an alternative you can also opt to also show a full Calendar in spinner mode by setting CalendarViewShown to true. The spinnerShown property can also be set to false to remove the spinners.

As well as playing with the way the DatePicker looks, you can also set and get all of the parts of a date using:

- DayOfMonth
- Month
- Year

You can also set and get maximum and minimum dates that the widget will show using properties.

When it comes to interacting with the widget you can set up a button to allow the user to set the date as with the TimePicker or you can use the OnDateChanged event to track the value. Doing this follows the same steps as for the OnTimeChanged event but with a small difference - there is no setOnDateChangedListener method. Instead there is an init method which can be used to set the date and the event handler.

For example, if you add a TextView to the bottom of the design surface and the following code for the event handler then you can see the date change each time the user makes a change:

```
DatePicker.OnDateChangedListener onDateChanged=
                    new DatePicker.OnDateChangedListener() {
  @Override
  public void onDateChanged(
        DatePicker view,
        int year,
        int monthOfYear,
        int dayOfMonth) {
  TextView tv = (TextView)findViewById(R.id.textView);
  tv.setText(Integer.toString(monthOfYear) +
                "/"+Integer.toString(dayOfMonth)+
                        "/"+Integer.toString(year)
  );
  }
};
```

To set up the DatePicker you need to add to the end of the OnCreate event handler:

```
DatePicker dp = (DatePicker)findViewById(R.id.datePicker);
dp.init(2015,20,2,onDateChanged);
```

which sets the year, month and day and the event handler. If you run the app you will see:

This tells you at once, February is selected and the date is 1/20/2015, that the months are numbered starting with Jan at zero not 1. The solution is to add one to the month number.

```java
import android.support.v7.app.AppCompatActivity;
import android.os.Bundle;
import android.view.Menu;
import android.view.MenuItem;
import android.widget.DatePicker;
import android.widget.TextView;
public class MainActivity extends AppCompatActivity {
@Override
 protected void onCreate(Bundle savedInstanceState)  {
  super.onCreate(savedInstanceState);
  setContentView(R.layout.activity_main);
  DatePicker dp = (DatePicker)findViewById(R.id.datePicker);
  dp.init(2014,4,2,onDateChanged);
  dp.setCalendarViewShown(false);
  dp.setSpinnersShown(true);
 }
 DatePicker.OnDateChangedListener onDateChanged=
     new DatePicker.OnDateChangedListener() {
  @Override
  public void onDateChanged(
     DatePicker view,
     int year,
     int monthOfYear,
     int dayOfMonth) {
   TextView tv = (TextView)findViewById(R.id.textView);
   tv.setText(Integer.toString(monthOfYear+1) +
      "/"+Integer.toString(dayOfMonth)+
      "/"+Integer.toString(year) );
  }
 };
}
```

Number Picker

You might be worried that the NumberPicker is going to be trouble when you notice that it is in the Advanced section of the toolbox palette! In reality it is very easy to use, all you have to do is select it and place it on the design surface. To try it out start a new project called Number and accept all of the defaults. If you have any problems with the rendering of the NumberPicker simply ignore the errors and build the project. The errors should then go away.

If you run the app then you will see the NumberPicker styled for the latest API which in this case looks very odd because there is nothing loaded into the spinner.

The reason for this is that the NumberPicker is slightly more complicated than the other Pickers in that it allows you to set what the spinner displays.

There are two distinct ways in which you can set the range that is displayed, as a pair of max/min values, or as the values stored in an array.

For example, if you just want the NumberPicker to show 0 to 9 you might use:

```
NumberPicker np= (NumberPicker) findViewById(R.id.numberPicker);
np.setMaxValue(9);
np.setMinValue(0);
```

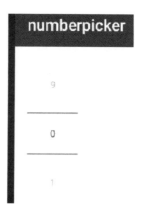

If you don't want the number spinner to wrap around you can use
```
np.setWrapSelectorWheel(false);
```

If you want to give the user the choice of 0, 10, 20 and so on up to 90 you first have to initialize a string array of the correct size for these values. In this case, the difference between MaxValue and MinValue properties plus 1 gives the number of elements in the list.

To create the array we need a simple for loop:

```
String[] values=new String[10];
for(int i=0;i<values.length;i++){
 values[i]=Integer.toString(i*10);
};
```

Once we have the array of values to display it can be assigned to the Picker using its setDisplayedValues method:

```
NumberPicker np=(NumberPicker) findViewById(R.id.numberPicker);
np.setMaxValue(values.length-1);
np.setMinValue(0);
np.setDisplayedValues(values);
```

You may have noticed that the array used to specify the values is a String array. What this means is that the NumberPicker, despite its name, can allow the user to pick from a list of arbitrary strings that you can set.

For example:

```
String[] values=new String[3];
values[0]="mike";
values[1]="sue";
values[2]="harry";
np.setMaxValue(values.length-1);
np.setMinValue(0);
np.setDisplayedValues(values);
```

produces:

When it comes to retrieving the data you can use the getValue method, which always returns an integer. This is either the index in the String array, or the actual value if you are not using a String array, of the item the user picked.

If you want to get a live update of the value the user selects you can use the OnValueChange event. The event handler:

```
public void onValueChange(
 NumberPicker picker,
 int oldVal,
 int newVal)
```

provides you with the NumberPicker object that the event occurred on as picker and the index of the old and new values. The only problem is getting the values from the String array that was used initially. This is probably not accessible from the event handler and may not even exist any longer. The solution is to use the NumberPicker's getDisplayedValues, which returns a String array of values currently loaded in the NumberPicker.

For example to transfer the value to a TextView you first have to define a Listener object which you can do easily with the help of Android Studio's autocomplete:

```
NumberPicker.OnValueChangeListener onValueChanged
                    =new NumberPicker.OnValueChangeListener() {
 @Override
 public void onValueChange(
      NumberPicker picker,
      int oldVal,
      int newVal) {
  String[] values=picker.getDisplayedValues();
  TextView tv= (TextView) findViewById(R.id.textView);
  tv.setText(values[newVal]);}
};
```

This uses the picker to get the array of displayed values, which it then transfers to the TextView using the newVal as an index. All you need to do to make this work is add the Listener to the NumberPicker:

```
np.setOnValueChangedListener(onValueChanged);
```

Now when your run the program the TextView is updated as soon as any changes are made.

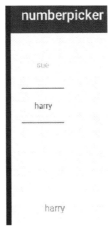

That's about all there is to basic use of the NumberPicker.

Multi-Digit Input

If you want to create a multi-digit input - for hundreds, tens, units, say - then simply use three NumberPickers. This is more tricky than it first appears if you want to dynamically track the current value across more than one NumberPicker. For example, to build a three-digit input you first need to place three NumberPickers on the design surface with ids numberPicker1, numberPicker2 and numberPicker3. Also add a TextView somewhere convenient:

You could initialize each of the NumberPickers in turn, but it is instructive to use an array of NumberPickers to do the job:

```
NumberPicker[] nps=new NumberPicker[3];
nps[0]= (NumberPicker) findViewById(R.id.numberPicker1);
nps[1]= (NumberPicker) findViewById(R.id.numberPicker2);
nps[2]= (NumberPicker) findViewById(R.id.numberPicker3);
```

Now we have an array of NumberPicker objects we can initialize them all in the same way using a for loop, but first we need the array of values:

```
String[] values=new String[10];
for(int i=0;i<values.length;i++){
 values[i]=Integer.toString(i);
}
```

As we are using 0 to 9 this could be done as an index without using an array, but this makes the example more general. Now we have the array of values we can initialize the NumberPickers:

```
for(int i=0;i<3;i++){
 nps[i].setMaxValue(values.length-1);
 nps[i].setMinValue(0);
 nps[i].setDisplayedValues(values);
 nps[i].setOnValueChangedListener(onValueChanged);
}
```

Notice that the same event handler is used for all of the NumberPickers. In some cases this is the way to do things, in others it is better to have an event handler for each widget. The next small problem is how to update the value displayed in a TextView when one of the NumberPickers changes its value. Again the simplest solution for an example is to get the values from each of the NumberPickers using a for loop:

```
NumberPicker.OnValueChangeListener onValueChanged
                    =new NumberPicker.OnValueChangeListener() {
@Override
public void onValueChange(
    NumberPicker picker,
    int oldVal,
    int newVal) {
 NumberPicker[] nps=new NumberPicker[3];
 nps[0]= (NumberPicker) findViewById(R.id.numberPicker1);
 nps[1]= (NumberPicker) findViewById(R.id.numberPicker2);
 nps[2]= (NumberPicker) findViewById(R.id.numberPicker3);
 String temp="";
 for(int i=0;i<3;i++){
  String[] values=nps[i].getDisplayedValues();
  temp=values[nps[i].getValue()]+temp;
 }
 TextView tv=(TextView)findViewById(R.id.textView);
 tv.setText(temp);}
};
```

In this case we don't use any of the event method's parameters, we simply find the three NumberPickers, then we get their DisplayedValues as a String array and finally the current value of each using the index returned by getValue.

The only tricky bit is building up the string of digits to be displayed in temp. If you aren't sure what is going on try changing the line that sets temp to read:

```
temp=temp+values[nps[i].getValue()];
```

In the jargon of math, String concatenation is not commutative but in the jargon of programming it matters which end of the String you append something new.

Of course, as all three NumberPickers share the same set of values, we really only need to getDisplayedValues once, but this is more general. Also it is very obvious that parts of the code are repeated and it would be better to refactor to create a function to get the three NumberPickers.

If you run the program, you should be able to alter what is displayed in the TextView in a sensible three-digit place value way:

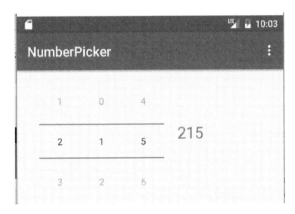

The complete program is:

```java
import android.support.v7.app.AppCompatActivity;
import android.os.Bundle;
import android.view.Menu;
import android.view.MenuItem;
import android.widget.NumberPicker;
import android.widget.TextView;

public class MainActivity extends AppCompatActivity {

  @Override
  protected void onCreate(Bundle savedInstanceState{
    super.onCreate(savedInstanceState);
    setContentView(R.layout.activity_main);

    NumberPicker.OnValueChangeListener onValueChanged
                       =new NumberPicker.OnValueChangeListener() {
      @Override
      public void onValueChange(
            NumberPicker picker,
            int oldVal,
            int newVal) {
      NumberPicker[] nps=new NumberPicker[3];
      nps[0]= (NumberPicker) findViewById(R.id.numberPicker1);
      nps[1]= (NumberPicker) findViewById(R.id.numberPicker2);
      nps[2]= (NumberPicker) findViewById(R.id.numberPicker3);
      String temp="";
      for(int i=0;i<3;i++){
        String[] values=nps[i].getDisplayedValues();
        temp=values[nps[i].getValue()]+temp;
      }
      TextView tv=(TextView) findViewById(R.id.textView);
      tv.setText(temp);
     }
    };

    String[] values=new String[10];
    for(int i=0;i<values.length;i++){
     values[i]=Integer.toString(i);
    }
    NumberPicker[] nps=new NumberPicker[3];
    nps[0]= (NumberPicker) findViewById(R.id.numberPicker1);
    nps[1]= (NumberPicker) findViewById(R.id.numberPicker2);
    nps[2]= (NumberPicker) findViewById(R.id.numberPicker3);
    for(int i=0;i<3;i++){
     nps[i].setMaxValue(values.length-1);
     nps[i].setMinValue(0);
     nps[i].setDisplayedValues(values);
     nps[i].setOnValueChangedListener(onValueChanged);
    }
  }
}
```

There is much more to say about the Pickers and how to customize them, but the methods explained here are the most common and customization generally only involves the use of fairly obvious properties and methods.

The biggest omission here is the use of the Pickers within a DialogFragment. This is a big topic that is covered in ***Android Programming: Mastering Fragments & Dialogs.***

Summary

- The Pickers - TimePicker, DatePicker and NumberPicker provide easy to use ways of getting user input without having to use an on-screen keyboard.

- Pickers are usually introduced as dialog boxes or dialog fragments. This is a good way to use them, but they are also useful if you don't use a dialog.

- With the introduction of Material Design with Android Lollipop, the look of the Pickers has changed. For easy backward compatibility use compatibility library v7, appcompat, which is included in your projects automatically by Android Studio, and stick with the AppCompat themes.

- If you stick with these defaults your app will use Material Design on Lollipop and later, but the Holo theme for earlier versions of Android. If you stray from AppCompat themes things tend not to work.

- It is possible and very easy to replace the Material Design with the Holo look on all versions of Android. Simply set the timePickerMode and/or datePickerMode properties to spinner. The NumberPicker always shows as a spinner.

- Use the OnXChangedListener event handler to respond to user input.

- The DatePicker in spinner form can also display a calendar using the CalendarViewShown property.

- The Designer isn't very stable. If it complains about missing classes or styles try ignoring the errors and running the project. This often clears the errors and allows the Pickers to render correctly.

ListView is probably the most commonly used UI component in an Android app. It isn't difficult to use, but you need to get to grips with the idea of an "adapter" and understanding what is going on pays dividends.

For a range of reasons, one of the most common things you need to do in an Android UI is to display a list of things that the user can select from. We have already looked at the basic Picker, but the ListView is a more general category of "picker".

If you are familiar with desktop development then you probably think of lists that the user can select from as being similar to a drop-down list. Android and portable devices often need something more than just a small list. Because of the limited screen size, it is often the case that the user can only be shown an overview of quite a few different items. When the user selects an item they are then presented with more details of the item, commonly called a details View.

Displaying lists and other collections of data is so common that Android has a mechanism that makes it easier once you understand how it all works.

The key idea is that to display a collection each item in the collection has somehow to be converted to an appropriate View object. It is the View object that the container displays for each item of data in the collection.

Understanding the Adapter

Displaying a collection of items has a number of similarities no matter what the collection of items are or what container is used. The container has various positions that are visible on the screen for displaying items. For example, a ListView has horizontal slots, one per item and a GridView has a 2D grid of slots. Each container accepts a View object and displays it in a slot. For example, you could provide the ListView with TextView objects and it would simply display text in each of its slots.

You might be wondering why not just supply a set of Strings to the ListView and let it work out how to display the Strings as text? Things could be organized in this way and it would be simpler, but only if you wanted to display Strings. If you wanted to display a list of images, say, then you would need a ListView that understood images and so on.

It is much more flexible to provide the container with a set of prepared View objects because then the container simply has to display the View object without having to perform any conversions.

All containers that derive from the AdapterView class make use of adapters to supply what they display in terms of View objects. As well as the ListView and GridView, they include the Spinner, Gallery and StackView.

We have already looked at the use of the Spinner and its associated adapter, so this time it is the turn of a more advanced UI element - the ListView and its adapter.

This approach also has the advantage that you can provide the container with a View object that is a complete layout, i.e. it could itself be a container with lots of View objects to display. For example, you could supply a ListView with a View object that contains an image and a TextView to create a multimedia list of pictures and text.

Of course if the container isn't doing the conversion from the data object to the View object - you are going to have to do it. This is where the Adapter comes in. The ListView and the GridView containers both make use of the ListAdapter class as their basic adapter.

Extending the ListAdapter Class

In general you have to take the ListAdapter class and extend it to create your own custom Adapter which generates a custom View object for the container to use in each of its slots. The container asks for the View object to be used to display item i or using whatever indexing suits the particular container. The Adapter returns the View object and the container displays it - without worrying what it is or what it corresponds to. This might sound complicated, but it turns out to be very simple in practice.

However to make things even simpler there is also an ArrayAdapter which lets you display a single text item for each element of an array of arbitrary objects. How can this possibly work if the object in the array can be anything? The first thing to point out is that ArrayAdapter is a generic class and can accept an array of any type as long as you specify it when you create the ArrayAdapter instance. The second point to note is that Array adapter calls each item's toString method to get some text to display in the container, which is very simple but also very restrictive. In fact, it is quite easy to modify what the ArrayAdapter displays and this makes it more versatile than you might expect and hence well worth getting to know.

Before proceeding a quick summary is helpful:

- Containers like ListView and GridView display View objects in a particular arrangement - as a vertical list or as a 2D grid in these two cases respectively.

- An Adapter converts the data that is to be displayed in each slot into a suitable View object.

- For complex data and displays you need to create a custom Adapter.

- In many cases the ArrayAdapter, a predefined custom Adapter for converting Arrays to TextView objects, can be used.

- The ArrayAdapter, at its most basic, can supply TextView objects to a container from an array of any type simply by calling the object's toString methods.

Using the ArrayAdapter

Rather then starting with an example that is completely general, it is worth looking at how the ArrayAdapter is used in conjunction with a ListView.

Start a new Android Studio project called ListViewExample based on a Basic Activity and accept all the defaults. For a simple example all we are going to do is display a list of names in a ListView.

First delete the usual "Hello World" textView. In the Designer scroll down the Palette until you can see the Containers and place a ListView on the design surface. At the moment the listView isn't automatically assigned an id. If this is the case type listView into the id in the Properties window. If you do this then a dummy content will be generated for you.

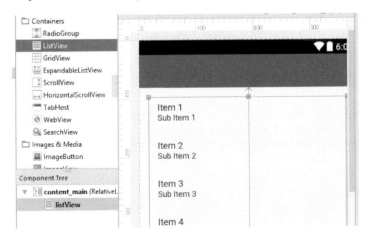

239

You will see that, for the sake of allowing you to work with the layout, the Designer show you the ListView filled with some two-item text objects.

Our Adapter is going to be simpler than this dummy display with just a single line of text.

If you run the program at this early stage you won't see anything in the ListView - it will be blank. The text that you see in the Designer is just to help you visualize the UI - there is no Adapter associated with the ListView and hence when you run it there is nothing to display.

Our next task is to create an ArrayAdapter object to supply the ListView with something to display. First, however, we need a String array to hold the text we are going to display. For simplicity we might as well add the code to the onCreate method in MyActivity.java.

To create a simple String array we can use a literal:

```
String[] myStringArray={"A","B","C"};
```

Feel free to think up something more creative than A, B, C. In the real world the Strings would probably be read from a file or a database, etc.

Now we can create the ArrayAdapter. To do this the constructor needs the context, usually this, and a layout to use to display each String and the String array:

```
ArrayAdapter<String> myAdapter=new ArrayAdapter<String>(
    this,
    android.R.layout.simple_list_item_1,
    myStringArray);
```

Notice the way that the type of the array is specified as <String>. If you are not familiar with Java generics then you need to look up how it all works. Also notice the use of the standard supplied layout simple_list_item1. You can create your own layouts and we will see how this is done in a moment.

Finally we need to associate the adapter with the ListView:

```
ListView myList= (ListView) findViewById(R.id.listView);
myList.setAdapter(myAdapter);
```

The complete onCreate method is:

```
protected void onCreate(Bundle savedInstanceState){
 super.onCreate(savedInstanceState);
 setContentView(R.layout.activity_main);
 String[]  myStringArray={"A","B","C"};
 ArrayAdapter<String> myAdapter=new ArrayAdapter<String>(
        this,
        android.R.layout.simple_list_item_1,
        myStringArray);
 ListView myList=(ListView) findViewById(R.id.listView);
 myList.setAdapter(myAdapter);
}
```

You will also have to remember to add import statements for each of the classes used - ListView and ArrayAdapter – easily done with Alt+Enter.

If you now run the program you will see a neat list with each array element displayed on a line.

So far this doesn't look impressive but the ListView gives you some basic facilities. For example, if you increase the number of elements in the array:

```
String[] myStringArray={"A","B","C","D","E","F","G","H","I","J"};
```

you will discover that you can automatically scroll through the list using the usual flick gesture.

Working With The Data

The whole point of showing the user a list of items is so that they can interact with it. You can manipulate the data on display in various ways and handle events when the user selects an item.

Get Selection

Perhaps the most important thing is to deal with the user selecting and item. The usual way of doing this is to write a handler for the OnItemClickListener, which passes four parameters:

```
onItemClick(AdapterView parent,View view,int position, long id)
```

The AdapterView is the complete View displayed by the container, the View is the View object the user selected, the position in the collection and the id is the item's id number in the container. For an ArrayAdapter the id is the same as the array index.

You can use this event to find out what the user has selected and modify it. For example the event handler:

```
AdapterView.OnItemClickListener
 mMessageClickedHandler =
   new AdapterView.OnItemClickListener() {
    public void onItemClick(AdapterView parent,
                            View v,
                            int position,
                            long id) {
  ((TextView)v).setText("selected");
 }
};
```

sets each item the user selects to "selected".

It is important to know that changing what the View object displays doesn't change the data stored in the associated data structure. That is, in this case setting a row to "selected" doesn't change the entry in the String array.

To set the handler to the ListView you would use:

```
myList.setOnItemClickListener(mMessageClickedHandler);
```

You can also set the selection in code using:

```
myList.setSelection(position);
```

where position is the zero based position of the item in the list and you can scroll to show any item using:

```
myList.smoothScrollToPosition(position);
```

A subtle point worth mentioning is that you can't make use of the View object that is passed to the event handler to display the selection in another part of the layout. A View object can only be in the layout hierarchy once. In most cases this isn't a problem because you can usually manually clone the View object. For example, in this case the View object is a TextView and so you can create a new TextView and set its Text property to be the same as the one in the list:

```
TextView w=new TextView(getApplicationContext());
w.setText( ((TextView)v).getText());
LinearLayout myLayout=(LinearLayout) findViewById(R.id.layout);
myLayout.addView(w);
```

This can be more of a nuisance if the View object is more complex.

Changing the Data

One of the slightly confusing things about using adapters is the relationship between what is displayed and what is in the underlying data structure. You can change the data, but if you want to see the change in the container you have to use an adapter notify method to tell that the data has changed.
For example, if you change an element of the array:

```
myStringArray[0]="newdata";
```

then nothing will show until you use:

```
ListView myList=(ListView) findViewById(R.id.listView);
ArrayAdapter myAdapt= (ArrayAdapter)myList.getAdapter();
myAdapt.notifyDataSetChanged();
```

Notice that you have to cast the ListAdapter returned from getAdapter to an ArrayAdapter to call the notify method.

There is a second way to change the data using the ArrayAdapter itself. This provides a number of methods to add, insert, clear, remove and even sort the data in the Adapter. The big problem is that if you use any of these then the underlying data structure associated with the Adapter has to support them. For example, the add method adds an object onto the end of the data structure but, with the program as currently set up, if you try:

```
myAdapt.add("new data");
```

the result will be a runtime crash. The reason is that in Java an array has a fixed size and the add method tries to add the item to the end of the array, which isn't possible.

If you want to add items to the end of an array-like data structure, you need to use an ArrayList and not just a simple array. An ArrayList can increase and decrease its size. For example we can create an ArrayList from out existing String array:

```
ArrayList<String> myArrayList= new ArrayList<String>();
```

and you can associate this new ArrayList with the adapter instead of the String array:

```
ArrayAdapter<String> myAdapter= new ArrayAdapter<String>(
            this,
            android.R.layout.simple_list_item_1,
            myArrayList);
```

Following this you can use:

```
myAdapt.add("new data");
```

and you will see the new data at the end of the displayed list. You may have to scroll to see it.

As long as you are using an ArrayList you are safe to use all of the adapter data modifying methods:

```
add(item)
addAll(item1,item2,item3...)
clear() //remove all data
insert(item,position)
remove(item)
```

You can also make use of:

```
getCount() //get number of elements
getItem(position) // get item
getItemId(position) //get item id
getPosition(item)
```

A Custom Layout

So far we have just made use of the system provided layout for the row. It is very easy to create your own layout file and set it so that it is used to render each row, but you need to keep in mind that the only data that will be displayed that is different on each row is derived from the item's toString method.

The simplest custom layout has to have just a single TextView widget which is used for each line. In fact this is so simple it has no advantage over the system supplied layout so this is really just to show how things work.

Use Android Studio to create a new layout in the standard layout directory and call it mylayout.xml. Use the Designer or text editor to create a layout with just a single TextView object. Create a new layout and accept any layout type for the initial file. You will can then place a TextView on the design surface. You won't be able to delete the layout however as the editor will not allow you to do it. Instead you need to switch to Text view and edit the file to remove the layout:

```xml
<?xml version="1.0" encoding="utf-8"?>
 <TextView
   xmlns:android="http://schemas.android.com/apk/res/android"
   android:text="TextView"
   android:layout_width="match_parent"
   android:layout_height="wrap_content"
   android:id="@+id/textView" />
```

Notice that you need the xmlns attribute to make sure that the android namespace is defined.

244

To use the layout you simply provide its resource id in the ArrayAdapter constructor:

```
ArrayAdapter<String> myAdapter= new ArrayAdapter<String>(
            this,
            R.layout.mylayout,
            myStringArray);
```

If you try this you won't see any huge difference between this and when you use the system layout android.R.layout.simple_list_item_1.

The next level up is to use a layout that has more than just a single TextView in it. The only complication in this case is that you have to provide not only the id of the layout but the id of the TextView in the layout that you want to use for the data. For example, create a layout with a horizontal LinearLayout and place a CheckBox, and two TextViews:

You can use this layout by creating the ArrayAdapter with:

```
ArrayAdapter<String> myAdapter= new ArrayAdapter<String>(
        this,
        R.layout.mylayout,
        R.id.textView2,
        myStringArray);
```

assuming that the TextView you want the data to appear in is textView2.

The result is a little more impressive than the previous example:

Notice that each of the View objects in the layout gives rise to a distinct instance per line. That is, your layout may only have had one CheckBox but the ListView has one per line. This means that when the user selects the line you can retrieve the setting of the CheckBox, say. It also means that a ListView can generate several View objects very quickly and this can be a drain on the system.

There are a few things that you need to know if you are going to successfully handle onItemClick events. The first is that your layout can't have any focusable or clickable Views. If it does then the even isn't raised and the handler just isn't called. The solution is to stop any View object in the container from being focusable by adding:

```
android:descendantFocusability="blocksDescendants"
```

to the LinearLayout or use the Property window to set it to blocksDescendants:

With this change the event handler should be called, but now you need to keep in mind that the View object passed as v in:

```
public void onItemClick(AdapterView parent,
  View v,
  int position,
  long id)
```

is the complete View object for the row and not just the TextView. That is, in the case of the example above it would be the LinearLayout plus all of its children.

You are going to work with the View object you have to access the objects it contains and you can do this is in the usual way.

For example:

```
AdapterView.OnItemClickListener mMessageClickedHandler =
                    new AdapterView.OnItemClickListener(){
 public void onItemClick(AdapterView parent,
     View v,
     int position,
     long id) {
        TextView myData = (TextView) v.findViewById(R.id.textView2);
        myData.setText("Selected");
     }
 };
```

Notice that you can use findViewById in the View that is returned.

A Custom ArrayAdapter

If you only want to display a String in each row you can use the standard ArrayAdapter and the object's toString method. You can even customize the object's toString method to display something different from the default, but it is still just a String.

If you have an array of general objects and want to display multiple items from each object, or items which are not Strings, then you need to create a custom ArrayAdapter. This isn't difficult, although there are one or two more advanced points to take note of.

For this first example, let's keep it as simple as possible. First we need some objects to hold the data we are going to display - a record type, say, with a field for name and one for number in stock, you could also add a photo of the item but in the spirit of keeping it simple a String and int are enough.

If you know other languages you might be thinking that we need a stuct or something similar. In Java there are no structs. If you want to create a record you create an object with the necessary properties.

Start a new project called CustomList and accept all the defaults. Navigate to the java folder, right-click and select New,Class. Call the class MyData and enter:

```
public class MyData {
 public String myTitle;
 public int myNum;
 public MyData(){
  super();
 }
 public MyData(String myTitle, int myNum) {
  super();
  this.myTitle = myTitle;
  this.myNum = myNum;
 }
}
```

The new class has two public fields myTitle and myNum and a custom constructor allowing us to initialize these fields. Adding this initialization constructor makes it easy to create arrays of the new class.

For example, in the onCreate method you can add;

```
MyData myDataArray[]=new MyData[]{
  new MyData("item1",10),
  new MyData("item2",20),
  new MyData("item3",30)
};
```

You might need to add more data than this to try out the ListView properly.

Now we have some data to display we need to add the custom adapter. Once again, right-click on the java folder and create a new class called MyAdapter, which has to inherit from ArrayAdapter:

```
public class MyAdapter extends ArrayAdapter<MyData> {
}
```

Notice that we want the generic ArrayAdapter to work with MyData objects. Most of the methods of ArrayAdapter will work perfectly well with arrays of arbitrary objects.

Next we need to add a suitable constructor based on the constructors that ArrayAdapter has. Android Studio can help. Right-click in the line declaring the class and select Generate, Constructor. You will see a list of possible constructors. The one we want to use is third in the list:

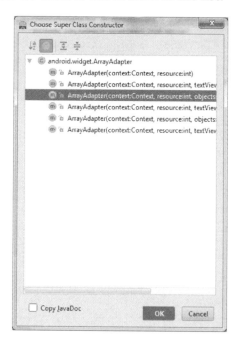

When you select it the following code is generated for you:

```
public MyAdapter(Context context,
                 int resource,
                 MyData[] objects) {
 super(context, resource, objects);
}
```

We need to extend this because we need to keep track of context, resource and the array of objects and first we need some variables to store them in:

```
private Context context;
private int resource;
private MyData[] objects;
```

The constructor can now store the values passed in to these variables:

```
public MyAdapter(Context context,
                 int resource,
                 MyData[] objects) {
 super(context, resource, objects);
 this.context=context;
 this.resource=resource;
 this.objects=objects;
}
```

Notice that with this constructor our adapter is used in the same way as in the previous example, that is we supply context, resource id and the array of data.

We now reach the key part of the customization, overriding the adapter's getView method. This is the core of the functionality of the adapter. Each time the ListView needs to display a new row it calls the adapter's getView method and expects to get back a View object that it can display as the row.

To override the method you can use Android Studio to generate some code. Right-click in the adapter class and select Generate, Override method and then select getView. The generated code isn't particularly helpful, but at least it gets the method signature correct:

```
@Override
public View getView(int position,
                    View convertView,
                    ViewGroup parent) {
 return super.getView(position,convertView,parent);
}
```

It really doesn't matter how getView generates the View object it is going to return, but the most common way of doing the job is to inflate a layout file.

To give the inflater something to work with right click on the res/layout folder and select New,Layout file. Call the file mylayout and change the LinearLayout to horizontal and add two TextViews with ids, title and number.

Feel free to change the layout to make things look pretty - it won't change the code you need to write.

Our first task is to get an inflater and inflate the layout file:

```
LayoutInflater inflater= ((Activity) context).getLayoutInflater();
View row=inflater.inflate(resource,parent,false);
```

Notice that we make use of the resource id we stored when the constructor ran and we use the parent View object passed in to the getView method. The only purpose the parent View object serves is to allow the system to layout the resource in a known container. The final false parameter tells the inflater not to add the resource generated object to the parent - this is a job for the ListView.

Before this happens we have to put the data into the View object. To do this we need to find the two TextView objects that we placed into the layout and this is just a matter of using the familiar findViewById pattern:

```
TextView title= (TextView) row.findViewById(R.id.title);
TextView number=(TextView) row.findViewById(R.id.number);
```

Once you have the View objects you need to change, you can use the position parameter to get the data from the array of objects that was set by the constructor:

```
title.setText((CharSequence) objects[position].myTitle);
number.setText(Integer.toString(objects[position].myNum));
```

All we need to do now is return the row View object:

```
 return row;
}
```

The complete myAdapter class is:

```
public class MyAdapter extends ArrayAdapter<MyData> {
 private Context context;
 private int resource;
 private MyData[] objects;
 public MyAdapter(Context context,
                  int resource,
                  MyData[] objects) {
  super(context, resource, objects);
  this.context=context;
  this.resource=resource;
  this.objects=objects;
 }
```

```
  @Override
  public View getView(int position,
                      View convertView,
                      ViewGroup parent) {
 LayoutInflater inflater=(( Activity) context).getLayoutInflater();
 View row=inflater.inflate(resource,parent,false);
 TextView title= (TextView) row.findViewById(R.id.title);
 TextView number=(TextView) row.findViewById(R.id.number);
 title.setText((CharSequence) objects[position].myTitle);
 number.setText(Integer.toString(objects[position].myNum));
 return row;
 }
}
```

Now all we have to do is write some code that makes use of the new class and this is exactly the same as the code that made use of the standard ListView:

```
MyAdapter myAdapter=new MyAdapter( this,
                        R.layout.mylayout,
                        myDataArray);
ListView myList = (ListView) findViewById(R.id.listview);
myList.setAdapter(myAdapter);
```

Don't forget to put a ListView component on the main layout.

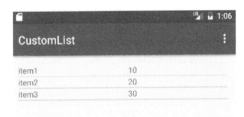

If you run the program you will now see a list consisting of two TextViews, each with something different to display on each line. In a real app you probably wouldn't create a new class for two text items, overriding the toString method would be easier, but the principles are the same no matter what the multiple View objects created by the adapter are.

Reuse, Caching and General Layouts

We have a working custom adapter class but there are some things we can do to make it better. The first relates to efficiency. If you recall it was pointed out that a big list of objects could result in the creation of a lot of View objects. In practice, however, we really only need the number of View object that correspond to rows actually being displayed on the screen.

To avoid having to dispose of and create new View objects all the time the ListView gives you the opportunity to recycle the View objects you have already created. This is what the convertView parameter in the getView method is all about. If it is null you have to inflate and create a new View object. If it is non-null then it is a View object ready to be used and you don't have to create a new one.

Modifying the previous example to make use of convertView is easy:

```
View row;
if(convertView==null) {
 LayoutInflater inflater = ((Activity) context).getLayoutInflater();
 row = inflater.inflate(resource, parent, false);
}else{
   row=convertView;
}
```

This is a speed-up worth making and saves having to create lots of View objects and dispose of them. However we are still looking up the child View objects every time we want to change the data:

```
TextView title= (TextView) row.findViewById(R.id.title);
TextView number=(TextView) row.findViewById(R.id.number);
```

This is also very wasteful and can be avoided with the application of the ViewHolder pattern. All we have to do is save the references to the children in an object and store this in the parent View's tag property. Then the next time we see the parent View we don't have to find the children we are looking for - they are stored in the parent's tag as a ViewHolder object.

First we need to create a ViewHolder object:

```
private static class ViewHolder {
 TextView title;
 TextView number;
}
```

Notice that this has fields capable of holding references to our two TextView objects. The logic of the getView method is now to also create and store a ViewHolder object if we are not recycling a View object:

```
View row;
ViewHolder viewHolder;
if (convertView == null) {
 viewHolder = new ViewHolder();
 LayoutInflater inflater = ((Activity) context).getLayoutInflater();
 row = inflater.inflate(resource, parent, false);
 viewHolder.title = (TextView) row.findViewById(R.id.title);
 viewHolder.number = (TextView) row.findViewById(R.id.number);
 row.setTag(viewHolder);
}
```

Notice that we have stored the references to the TextViews in the viewHolder and stored this in the row's Tag field - this is what tag fields are generally used for.

If we do have a recycled View object, we need to get the viewHolder object:

```
} else {
 row = convertView;
 viewHolder = (ViewHolder) convertView.getTag();
}
```

Finally, no matter where the viewHolder object came from, we just use it:

```
viewHolder.title.setText((CharSequence) objects[position].myTitle);
viewHolder.number.setText(Integer.toString(
                                    objects[position].myNum));

 return row;
}
```

With this change we have avoided creating a View object each time and we have avoided having to lookup the child objects each time, a very useful saving in time and resources.

Finally there is one last embellishment to apply. At the moment the layout for the row has to have the ids of the TextView objects set to title and number. It is much better to let the user set these in the constructor:

```
public MyAdapter(Context context,
                   int resource,
                   int resTitle,
                   int resNumber,
                   MyData[] objects) {
 super(context, resource, objects);
 this.context = context;
 this.resource = resource;
 this.textRes1= resTitle;
 this.resNumber = resNumber;
 this.objects = objects;
}
```

This constructor has two extra parameters used to specify the id numbers of the two ViewText objects in the layout. These are stored in private variables for later use and we need to declare the private variables:

```
private int resTitle;
private int resNumber;
```

The original constructor can still be used as long as it sets resTitle and resNumber:

```
public MyAdapter(Context context,
                   int resource,
                   MyData[] objects) {
 super(context, resource, objects);
 this.context = context;
 this.resource = resource;
 this.objects = objects;
 this.resTitle =R.id.title;
 this.resNumber =R.id.number;}
```

Finally we need to change the getView method to use the two new private variables:

```
viewHolder.title =  (TextView) row.findViewById(resTitle);
viewHolder.number = (TextView) row.findViewById(resNumber);
```

With these changes the adapter can be used as:

```
MyAdapter myAdapter=new MyAdapter(
  this,
  R.layout.mylayout,
  R.id.title,
  R.id.number,
  myDataArray);
```

and the user is free to use any ids for the layout as long are there are two TextViews.

There are aspects of the ListView that haven't been covered. In particular, what do you do if your data structure isn't an array? The ArrayAdapter can handle Lists by simply overriding the appropriate constructor. Anything more complex and you will have to create a custom Adapter. In most cases, however, this isn't necessary because most data structures can be mapped onto an array.

There are a range of formatting topics not covered, the header and separator for example, but these are relatively easy. More complicated are the multi-selection options and any custom list displays such as a list with multiple columns or pop-out detail windows.

Custom Adapter

Putting together all the code introduced so far gives:

```
public class MyAdapter extends ArrayAdapter<MyData> {
 private Context context;
 private int resource;
 private MyData[] objects;
 private int resTitle;
 private int resNumber;

 public MyAdapter(Context context,
                  int resource,
                  MyData[] objects) {
  super(context, resource, objects);
  this.context = context;
  this.resource = resource;
  this.objects = objects;
  this.resTitle =R.id.title;
  this.resNumber =R.id.number;
 }
```

```java
    public MyAdapter(Context context,
                     int resource,
                     int resTitle,
                     int resNumber,
                     MyData[] objects) {
     super(context, resource, objects);
     this.context = context;
     this.resource = resource;
     this.resTitle = resTitle;
     this.resNumber = resNumber;
     this.objects = objects;
    }

    private static class ViewHolder {
     TextView title;
     TextView number;
    }

    @Override
    public View getView(int position,
                        View convertView,
                        ViewGroup parent) {
     View row;
     ViewHolder viewHolder;
     if (convertView == null) {
      viewHolder = new ViewHolder();
      LayoutInflater inflater =
                  ((Activity) context).getLayoutInflater();
      row = inflater.inflate(resource,
                             parent,
                             false);
      viewHolder.title = (TextView) row.findViewById(resTitle);
      viewHolder.number = (TextView) row.findViewById(resNumber);
      row.setTag(viewHolder);
     } else {
      row = convertView;
      viewHolder = (ViewHolder) convertView.getTag();
     }
     viewHolder.title.setText((CharSequence)
                        objects[position].myTitle);
     viewHolder.number.setText(Integer.toString(
                        objects[position].myNum));

     return row;
    }
}
```

Summary

- Containers like ListView work together with an adapter to display data.

- The adapter accepts a data structure - usually an array or a list - and converts any data item into a View object that represents the data.

- You can handle a selection event to find out what the user has selected.

- The View object can be complex with an outer container and any number of child objects.

- The basic ArrayAdapter uses each object's toString method to provide the data to display in a ViewText object.

- If you want to display something other than the result of calling toString, you need to implement a custom ArrayAdapter. To do this you have to override the inherited getView method.

- The ListView is clever enough to provide you with View objects to recycle - although you don't have to if you don't want to.

- The ViewHolder pattern can make your use of nested View objects more efficient.

Index

18785580R00146

Printed in Great Britain
by Amazon